HOLLYWOOD'S
MADE-TO-ORDER-PUNKS

HOLLYWOOD'S
MADE-TO-ORDER-PUNKS
The Complete Film History of
The Dead End Kids
LITTLE TOUGH GUYS
East Side Kids
and Bowery Boys

by Richard Roat

BearManor Media
2010

Hollywood's Made-to-Order Punks:
The Dead End Kids, Little Tough Guys, East
Side Kids and the Bowery Boys
© 2010 Richard Roat

For information, address:

BearManor Media
P. O. Box 71426
Albany, GA 31708

bearmanormedia.com

Cover design by John Teehan

Typesetting and layout by John Teehan

Published in the USA by BearManor Media

ISBN—1-59393-467-X

Table of Contents

Foreword

by Mendi Koenig

As one of the last living East Side Kids, I was delighted and honored to be asked by Dick to write a foreword to his book on The Dead End Kids, East Side Kids and Bowery Boys. I thoroughly enjoyed Dick's biographical sketches of the gang. It brought laughter to my lips and tears to my eyes as I read about the gang of many years ago.

It has been my sincere pleasure meeting Dick and his family, and discussing his dedication to keeping these films of the '30s, '40s and '50s alive.

Contrary to the unknowing belief of many people who were really unfamiliar with these "B" pictures, we were *good* kids. We chased the bad guys, and every plot turned out well in the end.

True, we were a gang on film, but we were serious actors. As far as I can recollect, we did not get into too much trouble in our private lives.

Dick has a fantastic memory and a wealth of information, and brings to life so many guys that I knew and hung around with. Although most, if not all of them, have passed away (at this writing, I am 87 years old, and I was one of the youngest), they live on in Dick's book.

by Brandy Gorcey-Ziesemer

Contradictory, paradoxical, enigmatic. These are terms often employed to describe my late father, Leo Bernard Gorcey (1917-1969), who was known to millions as the feisty little ringleader of dozens of Hollywood Dead End Kid, East Side Kid, and Bowery Boy movies. I am convinced that the first five years of Dad's acting career (1935-1940) set the stage for his public and private patterns of self-destructive behavior at this time when he first gained public acclaim and national recognition. During these years as an immature and unsettled young man, he was cast into a public role as a tough Dead End Kid that overshadowed his own personality yet served his needs until it eventually consumed him. However much he came to despise this role, he never fully outgrew it.

In spite of my dad's turbulent and puzzling nature, I was never the target of his irrational outbursts. My memories are of a father who took me on long bicycle rides, took me out for ice-cream cones, read me bedtime stories and took me "uptown" where I was the center of attention as I sipped on a Shirley Temple while Dad enjoyed a stronger drink or two at any number of favorite taverns where locals in this rural neck of Northern California were mesmerized by Dad's celebrity. It saddens me that my siblings did not enjoy this side of my dad. I think the reason is because by the time I was born, he was retired and under a lot less stress and we spent a lot of time together while my mom did school and 4-H activities with the other kids. Whatever the reasons, I completely understand how unreasonable my dad could be and often was but feel very fortunate to have known and loved the side of him that could delight unconditionally in the antics of his youngest daughter.

Introduction

One night when I was about 12 years old (1964), I woke up to hear the television on, my parents had fallen asleep watching it. Since they were both asleep, I decided to watch what was on; little did I know that by watching the TV that night, it would be the start of a hobby that has lasted 44 years!

The movie was playing and some kid was running from the police. This caught my attention; I wanted to know *why* he was running from the police. Caught by the police, the kid was joined in a courtroom with five other kids. "Who were those other kids with him?" I thought.

I had to watch the whole movie, even though it was late. It intrigued me; I had to know the name of this picture and who these six kids were.

The next day I asked my dad if he knew anything about these kids and the movie I saw. He told me that they were the Dead End Kids and that he had seen them in the movies when he was a kid in the 1940s. I said to him, "You mean they made *more* movies?" I wanted to know all about them.

When I started this hobby some 44 years ago, I had no idea that I would be at this computer telling you, the reader, how it all began and of the people I have met.

I hope that you will enjoy reading about the kids and come away knowing more than you did before you turned the first page.

Hollywood's Made-to-Order Punks:
The Dead End Kids, Little Tough Guys, East Side Kids and The Bowery Boys

by Richard Roat, Jr.

Way back on October 28, 1935, at the Belasco Theatre in New York, a play called *Dead End* premiered, written by playwright Sidney Kingsley (also director) and produced by Norman Bel Geddes. Little did the two know that the play would have a run of 687 performances, lasting two years, making stars of six youngsters who would go on to be called the Dead End Kids.

With a cast of forty-six, including a dog, the storyline of the play was simple: it told of the injustice between rich, high-society snobs and the down-on-their-luck poor who lived within a stone's throw away from one another.

When the play *Awake and Sing* finished its run of 24 performances, on September 28, 1935 at the Belasco Theatre, work began immediately on the construction of the sets that were to be used in its next play, *Dead End*.

While the sets were being made, author Kingsley was busy trying to find the six young actors that would be the focus of his play. Already signed for the production, in the main roles, were Joseph Downing as "Baby Face" Martin; Theodore Newton as Gimpty, a crippled, out-of-work architect; Marjorie Main, Martin's mother; Sheila Trent as Francey, one-time girlfriend of "Baby Face"; Margaret Mullen as Kay, the rich girl Gimpty longs for; and Elspeth Eric as Drina, Tommy's poor sister.

For three weeks Kingsley searched high and low for his six young actors to portray his vision of slum-poor juveniles, going to radio stations, amateur theater companies and the Professional Children's School.

With help from producer Norman Bel Geddes, they chose twelve-year-old Bobby Jordan for the part of Angel. Second to be cast was 16-year-old Huntz Hall. Hall was given the part of Dippy when he auditioned for Kingsley and his imitation of a machine gun was better than another boy's. Fifteen-year-old Billy Halop would land the role of the leader of the kids, in the part of Tommy, giving up his job on radio as Bobby Benson. By the time Halop landed the lead in the play, he was earning $750 per week on the radio. The part of TB would go to sixteen-year-old Gabriel (Marcel Del Vecchio) Dell. For the part of "Spit," Kingsley cast newcomer Charles R. Duncan as the venomous juvenile who wasn't as tough as leader Tommy. Rounding out the cast was Bernard Punsly as Milty. Bernard was one of only two young actors with previous stage experience, the other being Bobby Jordan.

In the roles of the rival gang members, the Second Avenue Boys, Kingsley cast fourteen-year-old David Gorcey and older brother Leo (both understudies for main roles).

With the sets completed, depicting tenement housing of the poverty stricken and the rich snobs' high-rise dwellings, the orchestra pit made to look like the East River and the rehearsals all but over, the play *Dead End* opened on the night of October 28, 1935. Reviews of the play were positive; Kingsley and Norman Bel Geddes were given a three-minute standing ovation.

A look at life on the streets during the Depression in New York, *Dead End* focuses on how the choices of childhood, particularly in a community of people just barely getting by, can lead to the problems of adulthood.

The play focuses primarily on a gang of kids, who occupy the alley behind a wealthy apartment building, and a former Dead End Kid, "Baby Face Martin," who returns home with the law on his tail to see his mother and seek out the girl he left behind. "Baby Face" finds that he is not welcome. He meets another adult member of his former gang, Gimpty, now an out-of-work architect. It becomes clear to Gimpty that the best most of the Dead End Kids can aspire to is to end up like his childhood pal, "Baby Face" Martin.

There's also a somewhat love story between Gimpty and Kay, a woman who has ascended out of the slums by virtue of a relationship with a wealthy man.

The play reaches its climax when FBI agents kill Martin after Gimpty informs them of Martin's plans to kidnap the son of a wealthy businessman. Gimpty is given a reward for his information on the foiled kidnapping and offers the money to Drina, Tommy's sister, to prevent Tommy from going to reform school (and turning out like the killer "Baby Face" Martin), after he stabs the father of a small boy who comes to his son's defense when Tommy and the other boys beat and rob the small boy.

The film version of this play was to introduce the six kids to the movie-going public, they would be forever known as The Dead End Kids. Within days after arriving in Hollywood, the kids' antics, on and off the set, got the attention of the press. They bought old cars and raced them up and down the streets of Hollywood, Leo Gorcey receiving a number of citations, including serving a five-day jail sentence. On the set the kids refused to give the grown-up actors respect.

Director William Wyler originally wanted to film scenes on location on the streets of New York, but producer Samuel Goldwyn had his way and the film was shot on soundstages at the studio, with the sets being made by Richard Day.

After their success in *Angels with Dirty Faces* at Warners, Universal signed Huntz Hall, Billy Halop, Bernard Punsly and Gabriel Dell to contracts for the film *Little Tough Guy*. Little did Warners know it would be a year before they were to make another film with the kids.

Warner Brothers stepped in and re-signed the four actors to a five-picture deal (with an option for a sixth) and made a deal with Universal, giving them the sum of $100,000 for the kids' services.

Universal came up with a plan; they would begin a series of films called *The Little Tough Guys*. For this they needed to find six kid actors who could fit the mold similar to the Dead End Kids. They needed a leader to head the gang of kids and signed Frankie Thomas to do so. Already having Billy Benedict, Hally Chester and David Gorcey under contract, they needed to find two others. Harris Berger, who accompanied friend David Gorcey to a reading at Universal, was given a screen test and won the part of Sailor. Rounding the cast would be Charles Duncan, the original Spit from the play *Dead End,* as Monk.

A series of three films were made as *The Little Tough Guys*, the first one being *Little Tough Guys in Society* (1938), before they would join forces with The Dead End Kids.

The first film, billed as a D.E.K-L.T.G. entry, was *You're Not So Tough*, released in 1940. This was Bobby Jordan's first film back as a member of the gang, and missing were the services of Billy Benedict, Frankie Thomas (whose association with the kids would end in November 1939 with the release *On Dress Parade*) and Charles Duncan (who was in the military).

In the fall of 1939 Universal released the film *Call a Messenger* using Little Tough Guys, Benedict, Gorcey, Berger and Chester; this was the last time the four L.T.G. appeared together as a whole in a Dead End Kid picture. Dell, Punsly and Jordan were minus from this entry. They would not appear until the third film, *You're Not So Tough*.

The three *Little Tough Guy* films were done separately from the Dead End Kids, they stand out on their own and for this they are reviewed separately.

The brain child behind the East Side Kids, Sam Katzman (born July, 7, 1901, New York - died August 4, 1973, Los Angeles, California), got his start in films at the age of 13, working as a stage laborer on the East Coast. Eager to learn the film business from the ground up, he started as a gopher for Fox Film Corporation. Katzman quickly learned the angles of the low-budget studio, and soon became an assistant director. When cutbacks at the studio left him out of work, he became an independent producer with his first feature-length film, *His Private Secretary* in 1933, which he also wrote.

When Monogram Pictures, who made low-grade films, was sold by Katzman on the idea of a series of juvenile films in the cycle of the Dead End Kids, they quickly bought his idea. The East Side Kids films caught on almost immediately with the movie public, and soon after the first film was released, *The East Side Kids* (1940). The original East Side Kids were Donald Haines, Sam Edwards, Frankie Burke, Jack Edwards, Harris Berger, Eddie Brian, Hally Chester and David Durand. (Durand's part would be deleted from the final print.) Leo Gorcey, Bobby Jordan, David Gorcey, Sammy Morrison and Eugene Francis were added to the cast for the second feature, *Boys of the City*. Dropped from the original kids were Harris Berger, Sam Edwards, Jack Edwards and Eddie Brian. The third film in the series, *That Gang of Mine*, saw Frankie Burke and Hally Chester also leaving.

When Leo Gorcey wanted double his salary (per week) from Katzman in 1945, Katzman pulled the plug on The East Side Kids. Katzman soon after left Monogram for Columbia Pictures and produced the *Jungle Jim* adventures starring Johnny Weissmuller. (While doing these films, Katzman earned the nickname "Jungle Sam.")

The man behind the Bowery Boys was former cartoonist-turned-agent/producer Jan Grippo (1906-1988). When Sam Katzman pulled the plug on the East Side Kids in 1945, Grippo partnered up with then-client Leo Gorcey for the film series The Bowery Boys. Grippo would go on to produce 24 of the Bowery Boy features.

The Bowery Boy films were different from their predecessors. Whereas the Dead End Kid films were drama-oriented, the Bowery Boy films leaned heavily toward comedy.

Gorcey, as Terrence Aloysius "Slip" Mahoney, would be the leader of the boys, with his right-hand man being Horace Debussy "Sach" Jones, Huntz Hall. Added to the cast to make up the rest of the Bowery Boys were former Dead End Kids Bobby Jordan and Gabriel Dell. Also rounded up were former East Side Kids, Billy Benedict (Whitey) Bennie Bartlett (Butch), and David Gorcey (Chuck). When one of the gang would leave the series, their roles were filled by Jimmy Murphy, Eddie LeRoy and Buddy Gorman.

Home for the boys was Louie's Sweet Shop (located at 3rd and Canal Street, New York), where most of the action took place. The owner of the sweet shop, Louie Dumbrowski, played by Bernard Gorcey, was always there to bail the boys out with their IOUs for banana splits, or financing their latest venture.

The boys would travel to locals such as Baghdad, Africa, London, Paris or the Wild West. Whenever the boys found themselves in a jam that required fisticuffs, one of the boys would call out a "routine" number, which would tell the boys a specific fight plan.

Bobby Jordan was the first to leave the series in 1947 after the filming of *Bowery Buckaroos*, Gabriel Dell would leave the boys behind after 1950's *Blues Busters*, Billy Benedict left after *Crazy Over Horses* (1951), Buddy Gorman also left in 1951 (*Let's Go Navy*), and Bennie Bartlett left in 1955. Leo Gorcey would leave the Bowery Boy series in 1956 after filming was completed on *Crashing Las Vegas*. His heart and mind just weren't the same after his father Bernard passed away from injuries due to an auto accident on August 31, 1955. Bernard had passed away a week after the accident, on September 11. (David Gorcey and Huntz Hall would stay with the series until its end in 1958.)

Stanley Clements would take over the helm as the leader of the boys in the fall of 1956 for the next seven films. The series came to an end with the final film, *In the Money*, released in February of 1958.

Cast
Biographies

Bernard Punsly

Bernard Punsly was born in New York, on July 11, 1923. He began his acting career at the age of eight, on September 17, 1931, with a small part in the play *I Love an Actress* at the Times Square Theatre.

While attending school he answered a casting call for young actors to appear in the play *Dead End*, beating out seasoned stage performers, such as Bob Farrell, Philippe De Lacy, Richard Quine and Eugene Francis, and winning the part of Dead End Kid Milty. When the play *Dead End* was brought to the silver screen in 1937, Bernard reprised his role from the play.

Once in Hollywood, he enrolled at the Ken-Mar Professional School to complete his high-school education. His high-school yearbook reveals that "he likes the color blue— baseball and football——pretty girls! and the Glenn Miller Orchestra." His ambition, to "become a fine actor." Bernard graduated in 1940, with a double major, along with classmates Harris Berger, Florence Halop and Ethel Dell.

At the height of his acting career in 1938, his salary for the film *Angels with Dirty Faces* was $650

Portrait still of Punsly in film *Dead End*

per week. This year was also the only time that he acted in a non-Dead End Kid film, appearing in *The Big Broadcast of 1938*, playing the part of W.C. Fields' golf caddy.

With the completion of his last film, *Mug Town*, in 1943, he joined the Army Medical Corps, scoring high on his intelligence tests. He was encouraged to go to medical school, in the hopes of one day becoming a doctor. Upon being discharged from the military, Bernard enrolled in classes at the University of Georgia, Medical College, where he excelled and was AMA-Alpha Omega Alpha. After graduating in 1948, he served his internship from 1949 until 1950. From 1952-54, he completed his Residency in Internal Medicine at Los Angeles County Hospital.

Publicity portrait of Punsly for the film *Hit the Road*

In 1955 he became an active staff member at Torrance Memorial Hospital, Little Company Mary Hospital, Riviera Hospital (both in Torrance), and South Bay Community Hospital (Redondo Beach, California).

In 1950 he had married actress Marilyn (Lynne) Kufferman. The union produced two sons, Richard (1952-1996) and Brian (born in 1958). The latter became an Aerospace Engineer. Bernard Punsly retired from the medical practice in the late 1980s. He passed away on January 20, 2004.

Author's Note:

My first contact with Bernard came via a letter I sent to his mother in 1973. She told me that she would not forward my mail to him as he was too busy to answer fan mail. She told me not to bother her or her son because his acting career was in the past!

In 1979 I found an address for Bernard and wrote him a letter. I told him that I was coming to California, and I was going to meet with Huntz Hall and Gabe Dell, and to appear on *The Tomorrow Show* with them. He wrote back saying that he had some free time and would meet me for lunch.

When we met, we exchanged some photos and talked for about 40 minutes. Bernard said that he indeed liked being known as a one-time Dead End Kid, but it was also true that he now had a different life. One thing that he told me that I did not know, however, was that he had aspirations of one day becoming a director.

Over the next 25 years we kept in touch. He was a very gentle man.

Selected Filmography:
Dead End (1937, as Milt)
Dead End Kids films (1937- 1943, as Milty, Fats, Hunky, Ouch, Sleepy, Dutch, Ape, Lug, Butch, Creaseball Plunkett)
The Big Broadcast of 1938 (1938, as golf caddy)
On Dress Parade (1939, as Dutch)
Land of Liberty (1939, archive footage)
Junior Army (1942, as Cowboy)
Mug Town (1943, as Ape)

Stage Credits:
I Love an Actress (1931, as pageboy)
Dead End (1935-1936, as Milty)

TV Credits:
About Faces (1960, as himself)

Star, Hollywood Walk of Fame, February 1994

Billy Halop

Billy Halop was born in Brooklyn, New York, on February 11, 1920. His father Benjamin was a lawyer for the Trunz Meat Packing Company and moved his family of three children, Joel, Florence, Billy, and wife Lucille (Dancer) to Long Island in 1924.

In 1925, when Halop was five years old, and attending private school, a small radio station in New York met with school officials, asking to use the services of some of their students for a radio broadcast. Billy and his sister Florence were chosen, along with seven other students.

Having the taste of performing, the young Halop began going on auditions for radio programs, and was cast on shows like *The Children's Hour, Let's Pretend* and the serial *Home Sweet Home*. Billy's big break came in the fall of 1933 when he was cast in the title role on a CBS radio show, *Bobby Benson's Adventures (The H-Bar-O Rangers)*, playing a twelve-year-old cowboy. With the show being a hit with kids of all ages, Billy soon found himself touring the U.S., with the Colonel W.T. Johnson rodeo show.

By 1934, Billy had enrolled in the Children's Professional School for child actors, and started auditioning for stage plays.

Portrait of Halop from the 1937 film *Dead End*

When a casting call went out for child performers in the fall of 1935 for the play *Dead End*, Halop answered, winning the part of Tommy, leader of the Dead End Kids. With his previous work on radio, Halop was given his own dressing room, and considerably more money than the other kids, a fact that did not sit well with the others.

Dead End opened to rave reviews with the Dead End Kids—Halop (Tommy), Leo Gorcey (Spit), Huntz Hall (Dippy), Bernard Punsly (Milty), Gabriel Dell (TB), and Bobby Jordan (Angel)—getting most of the press.

In the spring of 1937, Samuel Goldwyn outbid David O. Selznick, paying $165,000 for the film rights of *Dead End*. Wanting to retain the realism of the play, Goldwyn cast all the kids in their original roles. With their star power from the film, Warner Brothers quickly signed the six kids to a contract.

Their first picture for Warners, *Crime School*, was released in May of 1938 and proved to be a box-office success. Not wanting to be typecast as just a Dead End Kid, Halop sought out other film roles, appearing in *You Can't Get Away with Murder* (1939) with Bogart, and *Dust Be My Destiny* (1939), with John Garfield. When his contract at Warner Brothers came to an end in 1939, Billy took his services to Universal Studios; it was the only door that was open.

From 1939 until 1943, Halop appeared in eight feature films and three 12-chapter serials as the leader of Universal's version of the Dead End Kids.

Being known as a Dead End Kid proved to be Halop's downfall, appearing in only a handful of films away from his Dead End Kid image, *Tom Brown's School Days* (1940) and *Blues in the Night* (1941)

After appearing in his last film, *Mug Town* (1943), as the leader of the Dead End Kids, Billy joined the Signal Corps, reaching the rank of Sergeant, being stationed in the Special Services unit in Europe.

Returning to civilian life in early 1946 and returning to Hollywood, Halop was given a screen test at PRC for the film *Detour*. After testing for the part a second time, the part was his, but three days before shooting was to begin, the studio had a change of heart and signed Tom Neal to a lesser salary.

PRC offered compensation with a starring role in a new series of films that they were launching called The Gas House Kids, a takeoff of the Dead End Kids films. Needing the income, he took the role, but not the series.

His movie career at a standstill, Halop tried his hand at marriage, marrying New York stage actress Helen Tupper in Las Vegas, Nevada, in May of 1946. The marriage would end in divorce a short time later in 1947. On February 14, 1948, Billy married for the second time, marrying Barbara Hoon, who was eight years older, in Palm Springs.

On December 7, 1947, Halop's movie career looked promising once again, with the release of the 20th Century-Fox film, *Dangerous Years*, where Bill received top billing. The movie made no impact and is only remembered today because of newcomer Marilyn Monroe's very small part as a waitress.

With a few minor parts in films such as *Challenge of the Range* (1949) and *Too Late for Tears* (1949), his film career was all but over. Drinking more and more each day finally led to a nervous breakdown and a suicide attempt. Bill found himself out of work once again.

With television becoming a new outlet, Billy began to find work, although still in smaller parts, appearing on shows such as *Racket Squad* (1952), *The Unexpected* (1952) and *Boston Blackie* (1953).

After filming an episode for the TV show *Robert Montgomery Presents* in 1954, the 34-year-old Halop called the Los Angeles Police Department, telling them that he had taken many sleeping pills, claiming that his wife, Barbara, had left him. He was also later booked on a drunk-driving charge, but received a suspended sentence.

Halop joined Alcoholics Anonymous in 1955 and recovered from his setback. He appeared in the film *Air Strike* (1955), with Stanley Clements, but it would be another year before he worked again, and seven years until his next film. Instead, Halop found work on such television shows like *Big Town* (1956) *Highway Patrol* (1959) and *Richard Diamond, Private Detective* (1959)

Halop's ten-year marriage came to an end in March of 1958. With no acting jobs coming his way, Billy began working as an electric dryer salesman (1958-59) for Leonard Appliance Company, where he received recognition and earned the title of Most Creative Salesman in the United States.

On December 17, 1960, Bill married the love of his life, Suzanne Roe, who was a victim of Multiple Sclerosis. By this time, Halop was working as a chef at "Ted's" Rancho Restaurant in Malibu, California.

Quitting his job as a chef a year later, the 40-year-old Halop enrolled in medical school, in the hopes of becoming a doctor. On the advice of his friend, former Dead End Kid, Bernard Punsly, that his age at the time played a big factor, Halop instead became a registered nurse, working at St. John's Hospital for the next three years.

With more and more acting jobs coming his way, Billy found himself appearing on such TV shows as *77 Sunset Strip* (1961) and *Going My Way* (1963), and the film *Boys' Night Out* (1962).

In 1967, with his marriage to Suzanne over, Halop moved from his home in Pacific Palisades to a trailer park in Malibu.

Billy's future was now in television, landing a recurring role as Pat the projectionist on the hit NBC TV show *Bracken's World* (1969-71). He found steady acting employment on such shows as *O'Hara, U.S. Treasury* (1971) and the made-for-TV film *The Phantom of Hollywood* (1974). In 1971 Halop was cast on the TV show *All in the Family*, as Bert Munson,

Publicity photo of Billy Halop for *Crime School* (1938)

the cab-driving friend of Archie Bunker; he would appear in nine episodes from 1971 to 1976.

Four weeks after filming the episode "Archie's Weighty Problem," in November of 1976, Billy Halop suffered a heart attack on November 7. At the time, open-heart surgery wasn't an option, and, on November 9, 1976, the Dead End Kid who never seemed to grab the brass ring, died in his sleep at the age of 56, at Mt. Sinai Memorial Park Hospital. He was survived by his mother Lucille, sister Florence and brother Joel.

Author's Note:

In going through some of my files on Billy, I came across a letter he wrote me, the first week of May 1976. In part, he was thanking me for sending him a photo of himself and Leo Gorcey that I had blown up to 7½ ft. by 10½ ft.

Billy stated that he had been working on his autobiography, to be called *There's No Dead End*, and that he was in the process of finding a publisher for the book.

He asked me, "Dick, I was wondering if you have a few pictures, like the ones that you have sent in the past to autograph. I don't have much from my days as a kid actor with the gang. In my life of many travels, things like photos have been lost or thrown away, seems I should have known better, but then I didn't know that I would ever write a book." He signed-off the letter, "Thanks for your loyalty, Bill."

Bill's book never saw publication.

A few weeks after Bill's passing, I received a package in the mail from Bill's sister Florence; the envelope contained the first 100 pages of Bill's book. A note from Florence said, "Bill wanted you to have this. My brother talked of you often and valued your friendship."

Selected Filmography:

Dead End (1937, Tommy)

Crime School (1938, Frankie Warren)

Angels with Dirty Faces (1938, Soapy)

Dead End Kids films (1938-43, Tony Marco, Billy Shafter, CadetMajor Rollins, Tommy Abraham Lincoln, Billy Barton, Billy Adams, Tom Barker, Billy 'Ace' Holden, Tommy Clark, Tommy Davis)

Swingtime in the Movies (1938, Himself)

Land of Liberty (1939, archive footage)

Call a Messenger (1939, Jimmy Hogan)

You Can't Get Away with Murder (1939, Johnny Stone)

Tom Brown's School Days (1940, Flashman)

You're Not So Tough (1940, Tommy Abraham Lincoln)

Dead End Kid films (1940-43, Ace Holden, Tommy Clark, Billy Barton, Tim Bryant, Tom Barker, Billy Adams, Tommy Davis)

Blues in the Night (1941, Peppi)

Junior Army (1942, Jimmie Fletcher)

Gas House Kids (1946, Tony Albertini)

Dangerous Years (1947, Danny Jones)

Too Late for Tears (1949, boat attendant)

Air Strike (1955, Lt. Cmdr. Orville Swanson)

Boys' Night Out (1962, elevator operator)

A Global Affair (1964, cab driver)

Mister Buddwing (1966, 2nd cab driver)

Fitzwilly (1967, restaurant owner)

Stage Credits:

Dead End (1935-1937, Tommy)

TV Credits:

Racket Squad (1952, Salesman)

The Cisco Kid (1953, Cass Rankin)

Highway Patrol (1959, Steve Dorn)

About Faces (1960, Himself)

77 Sunset Strip (1961, Tim Acton)

The Fugitive (1963, Mike)

The Andy Griffith Show (1963-65, Charlie)

Gunsmoke (1966-67, Bartender)

Adam-12 (1969, Judge Perkins)

Bracken's World (1969-71, Pat, Projectionist)

The Phantom of Hollywood (TVM, 1974, Studio Engineer)

All in the Family (1971-76, Bert Munson)

Star, Hollywood Walk of Fame - February 1994

Bobby Jordan

He could tap dance, sing, play the drums, saxophone and trumpet; the versatile Bobby Jordan was born on April 1, 1923, in White Plains, New York. At an early age, his mother recognized her son's gifts, and enrolled him in the Professional Children's School. With his boyish smile, it wasn't too long after that he was appearing in newspaper and magazine advertisements.

In 1930 he made his acting debut in the stage play *Street Scene*. One year later, he made his film debut in the short subject film series *Penrod*, playing the part of Sam Williams, Penrod's friend. He would play the part once more, later playing minor roles in the next six *Penrod* films, as a member of Penrod's gang. (The role of Sam would be taken over by David Gorcey in the series' third entry, *One Good Deed*, 1931.) The film series was filmed in New York.

In 1934, Jordan appeared briefly in the film *Kid Millions*, starring Eddie Cantor, filmed in California.

Back home and returning to his studies at the Professional Children's School, the young Bobby was spotted by playwright Sidney Kingsley, who was searching for young actors to appear in his play, *Dead End*. Through the school he answered the casting call and auditioned for the play. He won the part of Angel, the youngest and smallest of the Dead End Kids.

Bobby stayed with the play for little over a year, until November 1936 (because of school studies), returning in early 1937, just in time to go to Hollywood with the other cast members. (In Jordan's absence, his role of Angel was performed by George Levinson.)

Once in Hollywood, for the screen version of the play *Dead End*, 14-year-old Bobby was enrolled in the Ken-Mar Professional School for child actors by the studio, along with Gabriel Dell, Billy Halop, Huntz Hall and Bernard Punsly.

With the success of the film Dead End, Bobby and his fellow cast members were signed to contracts at Warner Brothers. In 1938, with the release of the first Dead End Kid film, *Crime School*, Bobby was signed to a new contract with the studio, as a solo performer, along with Leo Gorcey. The contracts for Punsly, Halop, Hall and Dell were dropped, but within four months of their dismissal the other boys' contacts were renewed with a pay increase, and the person responsible for their dismissal was fired.

In between his Dead End Kid films, Warner Brothers quickly put Jordan in the Edward G. Robinson film *A Slight Case of Murder* (1938), *My Bill* (1938) with Kay Francis, *Off the Record* (1939) with Pat O'Brien and Joan Blondell, and *Dust Be My Destiny* (1939) with John Garfield.

While on loan out from Warners, Jordan appeared in two Columbia feature films, *Reformatory* (1938), with Jack Holt, and *Military Academy* (1940), with Tommy Kelly, and MGM's *Young Tom Edison* (1940) with Mickey Rooney.

With the last Dead End Kid film made at Warner Brothers (*On Dress Parade*, 1939) and with his contract over, Bobby signed a movie deal with Universal, which called for him to appear in five Dead End Kid films at the studio. After the release of the Dead End Kid film *Give Us Wings* (1940), Jordan was able to renegotiate his contract, calling for him to make one film. He signed a contract with Sam Katzman to appear alongside Leo Gorcey in the film series the East Side Kids. Jordan fulfilled his obligations with Universal, appearing in the last Dead End Kid film, *Keep 'Em Slugging* (1943), in which he received top billing as the leader of the Dead End Kids.

Bobby would in 14 of the 22 East Side Kids films; his last, *Bowery Champs*, while on leave from the service, playing himself.

After filming the Universal serial, *Adventures of the Flying Cadets* with Billy Benedict and Johnny Downs, Jordan was drafted into the military as a foot soldier, serving in the 97th Infantry Division. Discharged in 1945, Jordan was involved in an elevator mishap, losing his right kneecap, causing him to use a cane for the rest of his life.

In 1946 he was offered a part in The Bowery Boys film series with Leo Gorcey and Huntz Hall. After appearing in the first eight Bowery Boy features, he left the series in 1947 not wanting to take a backseat to friends Gorcey and Hall.

Portrait of Bobby for the film *Dead End* (1937)

Now a freelancer, he appeared in *The Beginning or the End* (1947), *Treasure of Monte Cristo* (1949) with Glenn Langan, *The Fat Man* (1951), and his last film before turning to television, *The Man Is Armed* (1956) with Dane Clark. In the latter, he was listed tenth in the credits.

In between acting jobs Jordan found employment as a photograph salesman, rowdy for an oil driller, bartender (which proved to be his downfall) and for a short time he had a nightclub act, in which he sang and danced.

On March 12, 1946, Jordan married dress designer Lee Feruccio. Three years later, a son, Robert Carl, was born. The marriage ended in divorce in 1957 and Lee retained custody of Robert Jr.

In May of 1958 the out-of-work Jordan was jailed for being behind on child support payments, the press at the time pointing out that he had made more than a million dollars as an actor in his heyday and once lived in a $150,000 home.

From 1951 to 1965, Bobby had only a handful of acting jobs, appearing in small roles on such TV shows like *Adventures of Wild Bill Hickok* (1951), *Tales of the Wells Fargo* (1957), *Casey Jones* (1957), *Maverick* (1958), *77 Sunset Strip* (1959) and *Bonanza* (1961).

On August 25, 1965, Bobby was admitted to the Veterans Hospital in Sawtelle, California, and diagnosed with cirrhosis of the liver, brought on from his many years of drinking. Sixteen days later, on September 10, 1965, Angel of the Dead End Kids passed away at age 42.

Shot of Jordan for the film *Crime School* (1938)

Selected Filmography:

Snakes Alive (1931, Sam Williams)
Kid Millions (1934, Tourist)
Dead End (1937, Angel)
Crime School (1938, Lester "Squirt" Smith)
Swingtime in the Movies (1938, Himself)
Dead End Kids films (1938-1943, Swing, Angel, Joel "Joey" Richards, Bernie Smith, Cadet Ronny Morgan, Rap, Tommy Banning)
My Bill (1938, Reginald "Reggie" Colbrook Jr.)
Land of Liberty (1939, archive footage)
Young Tom Edison (1940, Joe "Joey" Dingle)
Boys of the City (1940, Danny Dolan)
East Side Kids films (1940-1944, Danny Graham, Danny Breslin, Danny Connors, Danny Stevens, Danny Lyons, Bobby Jordan)
Military Academy (1940, Dick Hall)
Junior Army (1942, Jockey)
Hedda Hopper's Hollywood No.4 (1942, Himself)
Adventures of the Flying Cadets (1943, Cadet Jinx Roberts)
Destroyer (1943, Crying Sailor)
Live Wires (1946, Bobby)
Bowery Boy films (1946-1947, Bobby)
Treasure of Monte Cristo (1949, Tony Torecelli)
The Man Is Armed (1956, Thorne)

Stage Credits:

Street Scene (1930, Charlie Hildebrand)
Dead End (1935-1936, Angel)

TV Credits:
 Adventures of Wild Bill Hickok (1951, Sandy Smith)
 Casey Jones (1957, Billy Mapes)
 Tales of Wells Fargo (1957, Bob Ford)
 Maverick (1958, Willy)
 77 Sunset Strip (1959, Auto Mechanic)
 About Faces (1960, Himself)
 Bonanza (1961, Thug #2)

Star, Hollywood Walk of Fame, February 1994

Gabriel Dell

Gabe Dell was born Gabriel Marcel Del Vecchio, on October 4, 1919, in Brooklyn, New York. His father, an Italian immigrant, wanted his son to grow up and become a doctor like himself, but Gabe had different ideas. Wanting to be a performer, Gabe made a deal with his father that if he earned good grades in all of his studies at school, his dad would enroll him in the Professional Children's School for child actors.

The young Gabe seemed destined for the world of entertainment, singing in the church choir and working on kid shows at radio station WWBC. While attending the Professional Children's School, he and his sister Ethel were cast in the play *The Good Earth*, but due to a paralysis epidemic, in which no child performers were permitted to appear on stage, their debuts on stage would happen two years later, with the play *Dead End*, in 1935. In *Dead End*, Gabe was cast as one of the Dead End Kids, T.B., and Ethel was part of the ensemble.

Publicity portrait of Dell for the film *Crime School* (1938)

In 1937, Gabe soon found himself in Hollywood in appearing in the screen adaptation of *Dead End*, being cast again as T.B. Working as one of the Dead End Kids, East Side Kids and Bowery Boys, Dell appeared in over 46 films as a member of the kids, his last being *Blues Busters* in 1950.

Branching out as an actor and away from the kids, Gabe appeared in the short subject *The Right Way* (1939), playing the part of Irene Rich's son. It wasn't until 1951 that he had another part away from the boys, appearing in the Ann Blyth film *Katie Did It*.

During World War II, Gabe was a member of the Merchant Marines, serving for a period of three-and-a-half years.

In between film appearances as one of the Bowery Boys, Gabe and Huntz Hall teamed up for a nightclub act in 1950, which resulted in wives Barbara (Dell) and Elsie (Hall) obtaining divorces in May 1953, telling the courts that the boys stayed out most nights!

Not wanting to be typecast as a Bowery Boy, Gabe set out to become a real actor, going back to New York to learn his craft. Dell went to the Actors Studio and would spend three years studying mime with Etienne Decroux and ballet with Jean-Louis.

In the mid-1950s, he married ballerina/actress Viola Essen, a fact that wouldn't be known for years. The union produced a son, Beau Del Vecchio, in 1956. That same year, the couple divorced.

In 1965 Gabe wed for the third time, to actress Allyson Daniell, daughter of character actor Henry Daniell, with son Gabriel Jr. being born two years later in 1967.

Moving over to television, after appearing on stage in the play *Ankles Aweigh* (1955), he became a regular on the *Steve Allen Show* (1956-61), joining cast members Don Knotts, Louie Nye and Tom Poston, where he was often called upon to do his impersonation of Bela Lugosi.

More roles beckoned for the small screen, appearing on such shows as *Armstrong Circle Theatre*, *Naked City*, and *Ben Casey*.

Back in New York during the mid-1960s, Dell appeared on stage in such productions as *The Sign in Sidney Brustein's Window* (1964-65), where he received rave reviews, *Luv* (1967) and *The Prisoner of Second Avenue* (1971).

Portrait of Gabe Dell for the serial *Junior G-Men* (1940)

Gabe returned to California in the spring of 1972 to star in his own television show, *The Corner Bar*; the show had a run of 15 episodes, ending in September of 1973.

Three years later and back in New York (1975), Dell's greatest success as an actor came in 1976 when he was nominated for a Tony Award, as Best Featured Actor, for the Broadway play *Lamppost Reunion*.

On the heels of his success on stage, Gabe was offered his own series on television, *Risko*; sadly, the series was not picked up for the upcoming fall season. A year before (1975), Dell had received star billing in the film *The Manchu Eagle Murder Caper Mystery*, as a private eye. Also in the cast was good friend Huntz Hall. Dell had also written this spoof of detective films of the 1940s.

Dell had roles in feature films such as *Earthquake* (1974) with Charlton Heston and *Framed* with Joe Don Baker.

Gabe Dell's last role as an actor came in 1980 in the film *The Escape Artist*; this film also marked the last time that he and friend Huntz Hall would work together.

On July 3, 1988, Gabriel Marcel Del Vecchio, the best actor of the Dead End Kids (as told to me in my conversations with David Gorcey, Huntz Hall, Frankie Thomas and Billy Halop), passed away in North Hollywood, California, at the age of 69, from Leukemia.

Author's Note:

Over a twenty-year period, which started with a letter in 1968, I was to have many conversations with Gabe. However, it wasn't until March of 1979 that we were to finally meet. On the day that we met, I appeared on the Tom Snyder show, as the founding member of a fan club devoted to the Dead End Kids.

After the taping of the show, Gabe, Huntz Hall and I went to dinner; we talked of my hobby, how they both got their start in the play *Dead End*, and how sometimes being a Dead End Kid worked against them when they outgrew their kid roles.

Huntz told the story of smashing up a car that the kids had bought. Gabe told of the time Leo Gorcey and he almost threw Bobby Jordan off a train going to Hollywood from New York to film *Dead End*. They also played baseball in the aisles of the train. When they arrived on the first day of shooting, they were fined by the studio one week's pay for misbehaving.

While attending the Ken-Mar School for child actors in California, Gabe Dell was elected entertainment chairman, also the senior class chairman, in 1938. Also on December 6, 1938, Gabe and the senior class all went to the roller derby with passes given by Gabe's pals, the Dead End Kids, with seats at the edge of the rink. Friends Huntz Hall and Hally Chester broadcasted the festivities. Afterwards, the Dead End Kids entertained the many seniors in attendance at Currie's Malt Shop, with Leo Gorcey and brother David performing a song-and-dance number, to everyone's delight.

From 1979 until about 1987 Gabe and I kept in touch with letters and phone calls. In July of 1988, I received a phone call from Billy Benedict informing me of Gabe's passing. Reverend Gary Hall, son of Huntz Hall, performed Gabe's funeral.

Selected Filmography:

Dead End (1937, T.B.)
Dead End Kid films (1937-42, T.B., Timothy "Bugs" Burke, String, Pasty, Ace, Luigi Petaren, Terry, Bilge)
Swingtime in the Movies (1938, Himself)
Land of Liberty (1939, archive footage)
The Right Way (1939, The Son)
Mr. Wise Guy (1942, Charlie Manning)
East Side Kids films (1942-45, Fritz Heinbach, Skid, Harry Wycoff, Dipps Nolan, Lefty, W.W. 'Fingers' Belmont, Jim Lindsay, Pete)
Spook Busters (1946, Gabe Moreno)
Bowery Boys films (1946-50, The Klondike Kid, police officer Gabe Moreno)
Katie Did It (1951, Eddie)
Who Is Harry Kellerman and Why Is He Saying Those Terrible Things About Me? (1971, Sidney Gill)
The 300 Year Weekend (1971, Wynter)
Earthquake (1974, Sal Amici)
Framed (1975, Vince Greeson)
The Manchu Eagle Murder Caper Mystery (1975, Malcolm)
The Escape Artist (1982, Uncle Burke)

Stage Credits:
Dead End (1935-37, T.B.)
Ankles Aweigh (1955, Spud)
Marathon '33 (1963-64, Al Marciano)
Anyone Can Whistle (1964, Comptroller Schub)
The Sign in Sidney Brustein's Window (1964-65, Sidney Brustein)
Luv (1966-67, Harry Berlin)
Something Different (1967-68, Phil Caponetti)
The Prisoner of Second Avenue (1971-73, Mel Edison)
Fun City (1972, Paul Martino)
Lamppost Reunion (1975, Fred Santora) (Tony Award nominee)

TV Credits:
Toast of the Town (1955, Himself)
Armstrong Circle Theatre (1956, Howard Mukluk Brown)
The Steve Allen Show (1957, Count Dracula)
The New Steve Allen Show (1961, Regular)
Naked City (1963, Willie Corbin)
Ben Casey (1965, Michael M. Francini)
The Fugitive (1967, Chester)
The Merv Griffin Show (1968, Himself)
CBS Playhouse (1969, Mickey)
The Corner Bar (1972-73, Harry Frant)
Risko (1976, Risko)
A Year at the Top (1977, Frederick J. Hanover)
Legends of the Superheroes (1979, Mordru)
The Tomorrow Show (1979, Himself)

Dialogue Director:
Joe Palooka in the Knockout (1947, as G. Joseph Dell)
Joe Palooka in Fighting Mad (1948, as G. Joseph Dell)
Joe Palooka in the Counterpunch (1949, as G. Joseph Dell)
Joe Palooka Meets Humphrey (1950, as G. Joseph Dell)
The Underworld Story (1950, as G. Joseph Dell)

Writer:
The Manchu Eagle Murder Caper Mystery (1975)

Misc.
Lookin' for Pop (documentary film by Gabriel Dell Jr., written by Gabriel Dell Jr. and Simon
    Stander-Independent Film, 2000)
Frankenstein and Dracula: Famous Monsters Speak on LP (record, written by Cherney Berg. Voices
    by Gabriel Dell)

Star, Hollywood Walk of Fame, February 1994

Huntz Hall

Born on August 15, 1919, Huntz began his career as an actor in the play *Thunder on the Left*, in 1920, as a baby.

After completing grade school at St. Stephen's grammar school, Hall, a boy soprano at the time with the Madison Square Quintette, enrolled in the Professional Children's School for aspiring young actors, after losing his singing voice while selling peanuts.

Also at this time, Huntz was heard on the radio in such shows as *Bobby Benson* (with Billy Halop), *The Rich Kid* and *The Life of Boxer Jimmy Braddock*.

In 1935, he had a chance meeting with actor Martin Gabel at the Children's Professional School. Gabel had just been cast in the role of Hunk in the play *Dead End*.

At first, Hall had auditioned for the role of Spit, but was turned down. At Gabel's urging, Hall answered a casting call for the play a second time. Hall immediately impressed Sidney Kingsley with his impersonation of a machine gun, causing the playwright to fire the actor who originally had the role of Dippy and hire Huntz on the spot. With all of his training, in tap dancing and singing lessons, it would be Hall's impersonation of a machine gun- "Hey, look at me, fellas, I got a machine gun, Yha Hea Hea Hea" - which made him an actor.

When Samuel Goldwyn decided to produce *Dead End* as a motion picture,

Publicity shot of Huntz Hall for the film *Dead End* (1937)

Huntz was signed with the others to recreate his stage role of Dippy in the film.

After completing the film *On Dress Parade* at Warner Brothers, Hall wed 18-year-old dancer Elsie May Anderson. They eloped to Yuma, Arizona, in 1940, divorcing in 1944.

Huntz Hall's first screen role away from the kids happened in 1939 with Humphrey Bogart in the film *Return of Doctor X*. From 1939 through 1943, Hall appeared in eight feature films and three serials as one of Universal's Dead End Kids, playing such characters as Pig, Pig Albert, Gyp, Toby Nelson and "Bolts" Larson.

Freelancing in September of 1941 and appearing in the Dead End Kid films at Universal, Hall signed on as a client of the Jan Grippo-Flo Brown talent agency. Grippo was representing Leo Gorcey at the time and persuaded Hall to join Gorcey in Sam Katzman's East Side Kids film series at Monogram Studios.

Hall's first film as an East Side Kid was *Bowery Blitzkrieg* (1941), in the role of Limpy. His name was changed to Glimpy for the next 16 films, until the series ended in 1945 with the release of *Come Out Fighting*.

Grippo proved to be a good agent, securing Huntz roles in films such as *Zis Boom Bah* (1941), *Private Buckaroo* (1942) and *Junior Army* (1942).

Hall received an honorable discharge from the Army, having only served one year. Before starring as Horace Debussy "Sach" Jones in the Bowery Boy film series in 1946, Hall appeared in two films, *Wonder Man* (1945) and *A Walk in the Sun*. Huntz playing a weary soldier in the latter film, receiving the New York Theatre Critics Circle Blue Ribbon award.

In 1946, Jan Grippo, now a producer, signed Huntz and Leo Gorcey to a long-term contract and started a new series of films for Monogram Studios called The Bowery Boys, with Gorcey as the leader and Hall as his right-hand man. By the time 1958 had rolled around, 48 feature films had been made.

When friend Gabe Dell left the Bowery Boys in 1950, he and Huntz formed a nightclub act called "Hall and Dell," with Gabe being the straight man and Huntz, his foil. The act consisted of them singing, dancing and doing old vaudeville routines. In 1946 Huntz wed costume designer Leslie Wright. Their son, Leslie Richard (later changed to Gary) was born on September 22, 1949. When the couple divorced in 1953, Leslie claimed that Huntz thought more of the act than of her.

Portrait of Huntz for the film *Give Us Wings* (1940)

Hall, like Leo Gorcey and Billy Halop, had his personal ups and downs in 1948. While at home one night and hearing noises outside, he phoned the police. No prowlers were found, but the police did find a few cans of marijuana, $200 worth, buried in his yard. Six months later, the charges against Hall were dropped.

Huntz would have two more run-ins with the police. He was arrested on assault charges for roughing up an apartment manager while attending the home of a friend. He paid a $50 fine and was released. In 1959 Hall was arrested again, this time for drunk driving.

Huntz cleaned up his act and participated in the Princess of Monaco Council for Drug Abuse, and enrolled in AA, completing their step program.

When Bowery Boy film series ended in 1958, Huntz went into semi-retirement, doing only a few guest appearances on *The Tonight Show* and the *Jerry Lester Show* in 1963.

Gary Hall and the author, March 2008

In 1965 Huntz married for the final time, to Leah. It was also at this time that Huntz found himself busy as an actor once again, appearing on two episodes of the television show *Flipper*. With newfound interest in his career, Huntz returned to the big screen in such films as *Second Fiddle to a Steel Guitar* (1966), with Leo Gorcey, and *Gentle Giant* (1967).

In 1971, Huntz was cast in the short-lived television show *The Chicago Teddy Bears* as a gangster named Dutch. The program premiered on September 17, 1971, producing only 13 episodes. He also appeared on friend Gabe Dell's TV show *The Corner Bar* as himself in 1972.

Throughout the '70s, '80s, and '90s, Huntz Hall worked nonstop in films and television, appearing in films like *Herbie Rides Again* (1974), *The Manchu Eagle Murder Caper Mystery* (1975), *Won Ton Ton, the Dog Who Saved Hollywood* (1976), *Valentino* (1977) and *Gas Pump Girls* (1979).

In 1993 Huntz was cast in the film *Auntie Lee's Meat Pies*, which told the story of four nieces helping their Aunt Lee make meat pies with a secret ingredient. This would be Huntz's last screen role before retiring.

On January 30, 1999, The Dead End Kid who could imitate a machine gun better than another boy passed away at age 80 from heart failure.

Author's Note:
In my last conversation with Huntz, by phone in October of 1998, he told me some things about his early years as a Dead End Kid, when the kids were making their films at Warner Brothers. "One day while on the set for the picture *Angels with Dirty Faces* the kids and I were introduced to a nineteen-year-old kid, who was going to school at UCLA College. The kid had just been given a job at the studio, this being his first day on the job. Part of his job was to pick up the kids' clothes from the laundry and run errands, attend to our personal business; his title was 'service boy.' The kid and I became lifelong friends; the kid passed away in 1972. The kid was Hall of Fame baseball player Jackie Robinson."

Huntz's son Gary is now The Very Reverend Gary Hall, Dean and President of Seabury-Western Theological Seminary, in Illinois. Costume designer Leslie Hall is now retired and living in California. Miss Hall designed clothes for the television shows *Get Smart*, *The Mary Tyler Moore Show*, *Lou Grant*, *The Bob Newhart Show*, *Camp Runamuck*, and the film *How to Succeed in Business Without Really Trying*.

Selected Filmography:
Dead End (1937, Dippy "Dip")
Crime School (1938, Richard 'Goofy' Slade)
Swingtime in the Movies (1938, Himself)
Dead End Kid films (1938-43, Pig, Crab, Huntz Garman, Cadet John 'Johnny' Cowboy, Gyp)
The Return of Doctor X (1939, Pinky)
Land of Liberty (1939, archive footage)
East Side Kids films (1943-45, Glimpy, Glimpy Stone, Glimpy McGleavey, Glimpy Williams, Glimpy Freedoff, Glimpy McClusky)
Zis Boom Bah (1941, Skeets Skillhorn)
Junior Army (1942, Bushy Thomas)
Wonder Man (1945, Sailor)
A Walk in the Sun (1945, Pvt. Carraway)
Bowery Boy films (1946-58, Horace Debussy "Sach" Jones)
Gentle Giant (1967, Dink Smith)
Herbie Rides Again (1974, Judge)
The Sky's the Limit (1975, Hitchhiker)
The Manchu Eagle Murder Caper Mystery (1975, Deputy Roy)
Valentino (1977, Jesse Lasky)
The Escape Artist (1982, Turnkey)
Auntie Lee's Meat Pies (1993, Farmer)

Stage Credits:

Thunder on the Left (1920, Baby)
Dead End (1935-37, Dippy 'Dip')

TV Credits:

About Faces (Himself)
Flipper (1966, Barney)
The Chicago Teddy Bears (1971, Dutch)
CHiPS (1978, Armored Truck Driver)
Diff'rent Strokes (1982, Happy Wanderer)
Night Heat (1988, Father O'Malley)
Daddy Dearest (1993, Pretzel Man)

Star, Hollywood Walk of Fame, February 1994

Leo B. Gorcey

Leo Bernard Gorcey had dreams of becoming a plumber, unlike his actor father Bernard. Leo was born June 3, 1917, in New York, to Josephine (Condon) and Bernard, following brother Fred (1915) and a third son, David (1921).

Leo's father Bernard earned a reputation as a successful actor with his performance in the play *Abie's Irish Rose*, and appearing in vaudeville shows. He spent much of his time traveling, leaving the discipline of the children to wife Josephine, who, being a devout Irish Catholic, insisted that her boys attend church regularly.

With Bernard's earnings as an actor, his sons dressed well and attended schools that offered highly acclaimed curricula; his three boys were secure and happy.

Shortly after the stock market crash of 1929, Josephine and Bernard divorced, with the separation being mutual, eventually reestablishing a friendship. Josephine would later marry an opera singer and have a daughter, Audrey.

By the time 1935 rolled around, Leo was in his last year of high school and working at his Uncle Rob's plumbing shop as an apprentice plumber earning six dollars a week.

With a day off from rehearsals of the play *Creeping Fire* (December 1935), Bernard accompanied youngest son David to the Belasco Theatre, to watch his son's rehearsals in the play *Dead End*. Leo had been told by his father and brother earlier in the

Gorcey in a pose for the film *Crime School* (1938)

day that he couldn't act, that acting wasn't for him, and they goaded him into showing up at the theatre. Leo, taking the bait, went to the theatre in his plumber work clothes.

When it came time for David to read his lines, Gene Lowe, who was in the scene with him, was in the bathroom. David urged Leo to take the script from him and read Lowe's lines as the Second Avenue Boy. Playwright Sidney Kingsley was so impressed with Leo's reading that Leo was given Gene Lowe's part; Lowe was demoted to an ensemble player.

Charles Duncan, in the original part of "Spit," came down with pneumonia after only three months in the role. Leo, as his understudy, moved into the role, leaving Duncan behind.

While filming *Hell's Kitchen*, Leo wed dancer Kay Marvis, on May 16, 1939, in Yuma, Arizona. The two had met a year earlier when Leo visited brother David at the Ken-Mar School for actors. The marriage doomed from the start; Kay wanting to be an actress, and Leo wanted a stay-at-home wife. The young couple, Kay, 18, and Gorcey, 22, divorced a short time later, in 1944. Kay did become an actress, appearing in a couple of East Side Kids films, *Kid Dynamite* (1943) and *Block Busters* (1944). Soon after their divorce became final, Marvis married comedian Groucho Marx in 1945.

In between pictures with the kids, Leo began to find work at other studios, appearing in *Portia on Trial* (Republic, 1937), the Buck Jones Western *Headin' East* (Columbia, 1937) and *Mannequin* (MGM, 1937) as Joan Crawford's brother.

Branching out more as an actor in 1939-41, away from the Dead End Kids, Gorcey had supporting roles in such films as *Private Detective* with Jane Wyman, *Invisible Stripes* with George Raft and *Angels with Broken Wings* with Gilbert Roland.

A year after becoming the leader, Ethelbert "Muggs" McGinnis, of the East Side Kid, Leo had the strangest role of his career as an actor, appearing as a native boy in the Bob Hope-Bing Crosby Road Picture *Road to Zanzibar* (1941).

With the East Side Kids films going strong at the box office, Leo got the chance to work alongside one of his favorite actors, Edward G. Robinson, in *Destroyer* (1943).

On October 24, 1945, the 27-year-old Gorcey married Evalene (Penny) Bankston. Three years later, Bankston filed for divorce. Needing evidence of Leo's drinking and cheating, and to gain more alimony, Bankston hired detectives to search their home. When the detectives entered the Gorcey home in Sherman Oaks, Leo, disturbed by their actions, and with gun in hand, fired three shots, luckily missing the detectives and Bankston. Gorcey was arrested on assault charges, with the charges being eventually dropped. Gorcey sued the detectives for illegal entry into his home, and was awarded $35,000.

While filming *Clancy Street Boys* in 1943, Leo met actress Amelita Ward, who would later become wife #3. The two would meet again, when Ward was cast in the Bowery Boy film *Smugglers' Cove* in 1948.

By this time, Gorcey and producer Jan Grippo had just finished filming the 10th film in the Bowery Boys film series, *Jinx Money* (1948). Soon after the release of *Smugglers' Cove*, Leo and Amelita were married in Ensenada, Mexico, on February 12, 1949. The marriage would last seven years, during which time son Leo Jr. (1949) and daughter Jan (1951-2000) were born. In February 1956 it was Gorcey who filed for divorce from Amelita, telling the courts that Ward had at least three affairs that he knew of. Amelita was awarded custody of the two children, and $750 a month in child support. Ward eventually gave up her custody of the children, but continued getting child support payments until she remarried.

Wanting to get away from the Hollywood scene after the death of his father Bernard in 1955, Leo bought a ranch (400 ft by 400ft) in Los Molinos, California, where he raised chickens and pigs. He married for the fourth time, to Brandy Jo, in 1956. She had been his children's nanny while

Gorcey had been married to Ward. Leo's second daughter, Brandy Jo, was born in 1958. But, by 1962, his marriage to Brandy had ended, due to Leo's increasing alcohol consumption.

He was now retired. Money was not a problem, as he was received $52,000 for each Bowery Boy picture he made plus 33% of the gross profits. Gorcey now had time to relax, write poems, and a screenplay, *The Candy Store*, which was never published. This proved to be Leo's downfall, as his drinking increased.

By the early sixties, Leo began to get restless and sought acting jobs, advertising in the trades. The first thing Leo appeared in was the *Dick Powell Show* (1962) in the episode "No Strings Attached." This led to a small part as a cab driver in the film *It's a Mad Mad Mad Mad World* in 1963. This would be his last acting part until 1966, when he and friend

Publicity portrait of Leo Gorcey for the film *Dead End* (1937)

Huntz Hall appeared together for the first time since 1956, as stagehands, in the film *Second Fiddle to a Steel Guitar*.

In February of 1968, Gorcey married for the fifth time, to Mary Gannon; it would be his last.

On June 3, 1969, Leo Gorcey passed away from liver failure, the day before his 52nd birthday.

Author's Note:

In 1967, at age fifteen, I wrote Leo a letter telling him how much of a fan I was and asked him for an autographed photo. About three months later, the photo arrived, as well as a short note saying, "Enjoy - Leo B. Gorcey." It was the only letter that I wrote him.

Selected Filmography:

Dead End (1937, Spit)
Headin' East (1937, Boy Boxer)
Mannequin (1937, Clifford Cassidy)
The Beloved Brat (1938, Spike Matz)
Swingtime in the Movies (1938, Himself)
Crime School (1938, Charles "Spike" Hawkins)

Dead End Kids films (1938-39, Bim, Spit, Gyp Haller, Leo 'Mousy' Finnegan, Shirley 'Slip' Duncan)
Land of Liberty (1939, archive footage)
Invisible Stripes (1939, Jimmy)
Hullabaloo (1940, Apartment house bellhop)
Gallant Sons (1940, 'Doc' Rearden)
Boys of the City (1940, Muggs McGinnis)
East Side Kids films (1940-45, Muggs Maloney, Ethelbert 'Muggs' McGinnis)
Out of the Fog (1941, Eddie)
Angels with Broken Wings (1941, Punchy Dorsey)
Road to Zanzibar (1941, Native Boy)
Sunday Punch (1942, Biff)
Born to Sing (1942, Snap Collins)
Destroyer (1943, Sarecky)
Midnight Manhunt (1945, Clutch Tracy)
Live Wires (1946, Terence Aloysius 'Slip' Mahoney)
Bowery Boy films (1946-56)
So This Is New York (1948, Sid Mercer)
It's a Mad Mad Mad Mad World (1963, First Cab Driver)
Second Fiddle to a Steel Guitar (1966, Leo)

Stage Credits:
Dead End (1936, Spit)

TV Credits:
About Faces (1960, Himself)
The Dick Powell Show (1962, Billy Vale)
The Tonight Show Starring Johnny Carson (1968, Himself)

Author:
Autobiography: *An Original Dead End Kid Presents: Dead End Yells, Wedding Bells, Cockle Shells and Dizzy Spells* (1967, published by Vantage Press)

Star, Hollywood Walk of Fame, February 1994

Bernard Gorcey

The father of Leo and David was born in Russia (of Swiss and Jewish descent) in 1888, emigrating to the U.S. in his early twenties, making his home in New York. In 1915, Bernard married fourteen-year-old Josephine Condon, and soon after their first child, Fred, was born, followed by Leo (1917) and David (1921).

After son Leo was born, Josephine left the *Ziegfeld Follies* as a dancer to raise her children, while Bernard continued to find work in vaudeville and in plays on Broadway.

By 1922 Bernard was cast in the part of Isaac Cohen in the Anne Nichol's Broadway production of *Abie's Irish Rose*, one of the longest-running plays of the day, running for 2,327 performances (1922-27). In 1928, he reprised his role in the silent screen version.

When son Leo went to Hollywood in 1937 to start a film career as an actor, Bernard and David followed in 1938. Once in Holly-wood, Bernard found acting parts in films like *The Great Dictator* (1940) with Charlie Chaplin, *Out of the Fog* (1941) with son Leo, and *Joan of Paris* (1942) with friend Paul Henried.

In 1946, with the debut of the first Bowery Boy film in the series, *Live Wires*, Bernard played the part of Jack Kane, before joining the series as a regular in the role of Louie Dumbrowski, sweet shop owner.

On September 11, 1955, Bernard (Louie, a.k.a. Louie the Lout) Gorcey passed away from injuries sustained from an auto accident.

Lobby card for the film *Abie's Irish Rose*

Dick Chandlee

Richard C. Chandlee, one-time East Side Kid, was born in California, in January 1923, to parents Harry and Edith.

Author's Note:
From this point on, Dick will tell his own story, written by him on March 20, 2008:

"My 'career' as a movie actor began at age 14 when I got my first job without really trying. I was brought up in the picture business. My father, Harry Chandlee, was a writer and motion picture story executive who had been active in the business since 1914. At this time, in 1937, he was working for Sol Lesser, an independent movie producer, who had an eight-year-old boy soprano under contract, a singing sensation named Bobby Breen.

"Sol's first Bobby Breen picture, *Let's Sing Again*, had been adequately successful and a second one, entitled *Make a Wish*, was to begin shooting shortly.

"One Sunday, Sol came to our home in Beverly Hills to confer with my father on the story for his next production. I happened to arrive at the front door just as Sol was having a last word with my father before leaving. I said Hi and we shook hands. I sup-

Dick Chandlee in a shot from *Clancy Street Boys*

pose you could call what I said next brash, but I meant it to be just humorously brash. I said, 'How would you like to make a lot of money?'

"Sol smiled and played along, 'Sure, tell me.' 'Put me in one of your movies,' I said brightly. Sol laughed. 'Not a bad idea.' He turned to my father and said that *Make a Wish* was scheduled to start in two weeks and the first stuff they'd be shooting was a boys' summer camp sequence on location at Malibu Lake, which is tucked away in the Santa Monica Mountains. 'Get Dick signed up and we'll make a million.' Sol smiled and left—and that's how I got my first job in the movies.

"They hired a good number of boys to fill out the camp sequence and I was just one of them. I saw the movie after it was released, and I don't think I was able to find myself in a single shot. But that wasn't the last time that would happen.

"I joined the Screen Actors Guild and got an agent, a middle-aged heavyset woman named Lola Moore, who specialized in representing kids of all ages. She was able to get me a number of small parts and day-player jobs, having only a couple of speaking lines.

"Then, finally, at age 16, in 1940, I got a supporting role in an RKO production called *Tom Brown's School Days*. When the picture was released, I finally got a chance to see myself perform as a movie actor. I thought I did OK but, well, you know…

"All this led me to the Jan Grippo and Flo Brown agency. I was now the responsibility of Grippo. In January 1943, Grippo called me and said to get over to Monogram Studios as quick as possible, 'They're waiting for you!' I got there and was cast as one of the gang in an East Side Kids picture entitled *Clancy Street Boys*.

"*Clancy Street Boys* was my last civilian movie-acting experience. In February 1943, I was inducted into the Army and was lucky enough to be assigned to the Army Air Forces. I did some movie stuff while in the Army, including an Army training film with Ronald Reagan, and one with a young Robert Mitchum.

"Before being honorably discharged in February 1946, I appeared in the play *Winged Victory* at the 44th Street Theatre in New York. The play was produced by The U.S. Army Air Forces.

"The play opened on November 20, 1943, and had a run of 212 performances, closing on May 20, 1944; I was billed as Pfc. Dick Chandlee, along with 280 other servicemen. The Andrew Sisters and Carmen Miranda sang all the songs; us soldiers, we sang backup.

"On July 20, 1946, I married Truda, a really magnificent woman. Our son, Christopher, was born in 1950. Truda and I were married for a total of 58 years before she passed away.

Dick and wife Truda

"From 1965, until I retired in 1992, I was employed at NASA's Jet Propulsion Laboratory with the Stardust Outreach Team, as a writer, explaining subjects like deep space communications and the search for extraterrestrial intelligence."

Dick, now in semi-retirement, makes his home in Burbank, California; he is presently writing his autobiography. In his spare time, he enjoys tinkering on his 1965 Ford Mustang.

Author's Note:

Over the past twenty-five years, I have talked to Dick many times about his life in and out of films; one particular conversation comes to mind from 1994. "One evening, in February of 1943, three or four of my Air Force buddies got passes and went into town [Fresno, California] for some food and fun," Dick told me. "We were walking from a bus stop down a street toward the center of town when one of the guys yelled, 'Hey, Dick!' I turned to see him pointing at a full-size billboard we were approaching. 'Isn't that you?' I looked, and sure enough, it was a great big picture ad for the coming of *Clancy Street Boys*, a shot of 'the gang' holding up a horizontal Leo Gorcey with a comic-surprise look on his face, and my face and everyone else. Now I was a celebrity, the only guy in the local Air Force who had a movie playing in the neighborhood, at least for an upcoming week or so.

Filmography:
Tom Brown's School Days (1940, Tadpole Martin)
Nothing But the Truth (1941, Office Boy)
I Was Framed (1942, Office Boy)
Murder in the Big House (1942, Newsboy)
Yankee Doodle Dandy (1942, Teenager)
The Major and the Minor (1942, Cadet)
Henry Aldrich, Editor (1942, Student)
Keep 'em Slugging (1943, Sammy)
She Has What it Takes (1943, Western Union Boy)
Clancy Street Boys (1943, Stash)
Henry Aldrich Gets Glamour (1943, Droop)
We've Never Been Licked (1943, Student)

Stage Credits:
Winged Victory (1943-44, Pfc. Dick Chandlee)

Mendie Koenig

Mendie was born in May of 1920, on New York's Lower East Side, to immigrant parents, experiencing all the typical activities that New York kids did, as depicted in some East Side Kids movies.

His father, who was a wanderer, always seeking a better place to live, decided to take the family out the squalor of New York City. He had first wandered to Cleveland, Ohio, where two of his older siblings were born, followed by stints in New Jersey, Philadelphia Pa., Seattle, Washington, San Francisco, California, returning to New York each time. He finally decided to settle his family in Los Angeles, California.

His family, consisting of five children, spent seven days on the All American bus line; these were the days before freeways. Mendie's parents, always poor, had eighty dollars to "settle" in their new home.

Mendie graduated from Roosevelt High School in 1938, after completing two years of high school in New York. After graduation, he attended Los Angeles City College from 1938 to 1940, completing comprehensive drama courses in speech, pantomime, direction, stage movements, stage construction, etc. One of his many partners in his drama class was a girl from the Midwest named Donna Mullinger, who later became known to the world as Donna Reed.

From 1940 to 1943, he used his drama training to participate and appear in many legitimate shows and experimental plays with Alexis Smith. Opportunity was knocking and he heard it loud and clear.

Needing regular income, Mendie took a job as a clerk with the U.S. Engineers; soon

Photo of Mendie from the 1940s

after, word came to the U.S. Engineers that help was needed on the Costa Rica segment of a highway being built, and, instead of being drafted into the Army, Mendie enlisted. He was assigned to San Jose, Costa Rica, and became the head of the payroll department for military and private employees working on the highway in Panama and Costa Rica.

After about a year in the Army, being a skinny kid, and not cut out for the rigors of Army life, he was honorably discharged.

Getting into films was a difficult task, no could get a movie job unless they belonged to the Screen Actors Guild, and no one could get into the Screen Actors Guild unless they had a part in a film—it was a Catch-22. Being inexperienced, but determined, he learned the ropes and auditioned for the film *River Gang*, and won the part. Being spotted in this role, he was cast as one of the East Side Kids in the part of Danny Moore or Sammy. It was also at this time that he was cast in *Youth for the Kingdom*, a Lutheran Church film.

In between pictures, he was called for interviews at some major studios, but getting the same response from all of them: "Mendie, when we need a street tough kid, we'll call you." He was typecast. One such role that he was up for was in the film *Killer McCoy*, with Mickey Rooney, but he lost the part to friend David Gorcey.

Feeling that he was more qualified and experienced to play more mature roles, friend Gerald S. Herdan was able to find him work at Roland Reed Productions, an independent movie-producing company. For them he did a number of rehabilitative films for the U.S. Military. Some of the roles called for him to be a wounded soldier, sailor, or Marine, the camera following him from being wounded through all the steps of being rehabilitated. He played burned military personnel, soldiers with lost limbs, and other various war mishaps.

In 1946 he enrolled in photography school, under the G.I. Bill, and became a photographer, he was in business for himself and subsequently worked for a photo studio, taking children's pictures. He also married the love of his life, Esther; a union that would last for over 50 years.

Going back to school, Mendie found his true calling, receiving a degree in teaching, graduating in 1951 from Cal State, Northridge. He worked for the Los Angeles Unified School District, rising to the rank of principal in 1972, and retiring from this position in 1987 at the age of 67.

Mendie is now retired and living in the Los Angeles area. Daughter Yvonne is a third-grade teacher for the Los Angeles school district and son Eric is the director of student affairs at the University of California at San Francisco U.C.S.F., both following in their father's footsteps.

Author's Note

I became friends with Mendie sometime in late 1984 when I wrote him a letter. Our friendship is something that I cherish very much. He is the kindest person I have ever met.

Mendie and I see one another at least twice a year in Las Vegas, at the Paris Hotel, when we meet on Tuesday afternoons for lunch. Our meetings are spent talking of the old days and the actors that he worked with. He is a wealth of information and every sentence is filled with much anticipation. Two of the many stories that Mendie has told me are my favorites:

"One day, I was relaxing on the set, waiting for my next scene, when I became aware of people visiting the filming. This was an everyday practice, inviting visitors. They were cautioned that when they heard, 'okay,' we are ready to shoot, quiet on the set! It was directed at them as well as the crew. During the setting-up period, they were invited to mingle with the cast. One gentleman was squiring a group of teenagers, and was announcing to them that he had the pleasure of becoming acquainted with Bobby Breen, the child actor/singer. He went on and elaborated about his friendship with Bobby, which interested me. He said this was in Chicago. His audience was attentive and interested.

"Imagine my surprise, when he put his hand on my shoulder as he was relating all of this, and saying to me, 'Bobby, it is good to see you again.'

"It took me a few moments to recover, and discover he was introducing me as Bobby Breen, whom I have never met, and who I don't resemble. All of the group approached me, and looked at me with awe. I didn't say anything for fear of contradicting or spoiling his story. I just grinned and waved.

"He whipped out a piece of paper and pen, and asked me to sign my autograph. I obliged, and wrote, 'So good to see you again,' and I signed it…Bobby Breen.

"In 1938, I was 18 years old, attending L.A. City College, and taking courses such as advertising, salesmanship, bookkeeping, etc. It was the end of the semester, and I was going home on the 'B' streetcar to where I lived with my parents in Boyle Heights, Los Angeles.

Mendie and wife Esther

"I was feeling pretty blue and frustrated; I was not happy with what was happening as far as my education was concerned. I wasn't excited or enthused about the courses I was taking. I didn't want to quit school, and I didn't know what to do.

"On the streetcar was Aaron Rellossoroff; we were not really good friends, just casual friends, Aaron was watching me, he came over and sat next to me. He inquired about what was troubling me. I am telling all of this in detail, because this was the turning point of my young life.

"I explained to Aaron how I felt, he listened carefully. He said, 'Mendie, why don't you switch to drama courses? You would be a natural. Well, you're always joking and clowning around…You make people laugh…you would be a natural actor.'

"The next day I changed my major to the arts."

Mendie is a star each and every Tuesday, not of the slot machines, where he can be found. Everyone knows his name and he is treated like the star that he is.

Filmography:
Docks of New York (1945, Sam)
Youth for the Kingdom (1945, Joe)
Mr. Muggs Rides Again (1945, Sam)
River Gang (1945, Butch)
Come Out Fighting (1945, Danny Moore)

Stage Credits (1938-43)

On the Level (singing/dancing)

Leave it to Smith (English Butler)

The Mountains Come to the Goldstein's (75-year-old man, when he was 23 at time)

Pygmalion (Cockney character)

The Man Who Came to Dinner (Banjo)

The Time of Your Life (comedian/dancer)

Spring Green (boy with fire-red hair)

Halley Chester

Hally Chester was born on March 6, 1921, in Brooklyn, New York. As a youngster of fourteen (1935), he auditioned for a part in the Broadway production of the play *Dead End*, but was turned down, along with Eugene Francis. Two years later, he auditioned again and was cast as an ensemble player. When *Dead End* took to the road for a coast-to-coast tour, with a stop in California, Chester quit the show along with Harris Berger and David Gorcey.

Once in California, Chester enrolled at the Ken-Mar Professional School for movie children and retained an agent for film work.

In 1938 he made his screen debut in the film *Crime School* as a reform school inmate. His part was not credited.

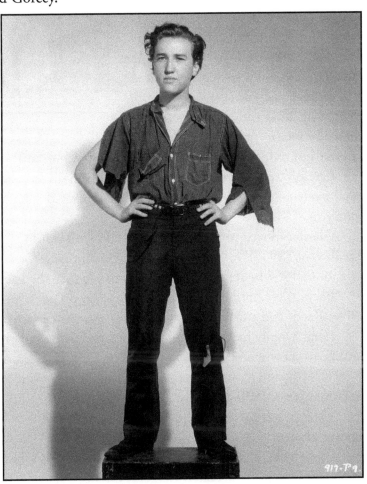

On the advice from friend David Gorcey, Chester went on a casting call at Universal for a part in the film *Little Tough Guy* (1938). Chester, along with Gorcey, was signed to a contract, for this film and subsequently was signed to a contract at Universal to appear in a series of films that the studio was launching called *The Little Tough Guys*.

While on loan out from Universal, Chester appeared in the Colombia feature film *Juvenile Court* (1938). He also appeared in *Personal Secretary* (1938), *Off the Record* (1939, with Bobby Jordan), *When Tomorrow Comes* (1939) and *The Witness Vanishes* (1939), before becoming one of the original East Side Kids in 1940.

While on a personal appearance tour with the Dead End Kids, the long-haired,

Chester strikes a pose for the film *Little Tough Guy* (1938)

fast-taking Hally Chester disclosed at his 21st birthday celebration at the Florentine Gardens (New Jersey) that he had wed Peggy Garrick, of Roundup, Montana, on December 17, 1940, in Biddeford, Maine. The two had met in Boston the year before when Chester was on a personal appearance tour and Miss Garrick was attending boarding school.

Hally Chester as Dope in *Little Tough Guy* (1938)

When Sam Katzman started the East Side Kid film series in 1940, he cast Chester as one of the leads in the first picture, *The East Side Kids*, in the part of Fred 'Dutch' Kuhn. Chester would only make one other film as an East Side Kid, *Boys of the City* (1940), before becoming a producer.

Chester's first film as a producer was *Joe Palooka, Champ* (1946). Nine more films followed in the series, starring Joe Kirkwood Jr. as boxer Joe Palooka, with titles such as *Joe Palooka in Knockout* and *Joe Palooka in the Big Fight*. The final film in the series was *Joe Palooka in Triple Cross* (1951).

Chester not only was the producer of the series, but he also wrote the stories for each one.

Chester marriage to Peggy Garrick ended in divorce, and on July 21, 1946 he married former actress Ethel Evelyne, in Las Vegas Nevada. They separated soon after, in May of 1947, and were divorced the same year.

Chester moved to England in the 1956 with third wife, Virginia, and kept busy producing films like *The Weapon* (1957), *School for Scoundrels* (1960), and *The Double Man* (1967) with Yul Brynner and Britt Ekland. In 1968 he returned to the U.S. to produce the Paul Newman film *The Secret War of Harry Frigg*.

Back to his home in England, he produced *Take a Girl Like You* (1970), starring Hayley Mills and Oliver Reed, and thirty years later (2000) was the executive producer for the TV version.

Long happily married and now retired and living in London with wife Virginia, Hally devotes most of his time to snow skiing and golf, and time on their 35-foot cabin cruiser, which is moored in Cannes, France.

The Chesters have two grown sons, Timothy and Mark; a third son, Steven, was killed in an auto accident on November 4, 1978, at the age of 24.

Author's Note:

Classmates of Hally Chester, at the Ken-Mar School in Hollywood, were David Gorcey, Billy Halop, Bobby Jordan, Harris Berger, Florence Halop, Charles Duncan, Bernard Punsly, Gabriel Dell and sister Ethel.

All of my efforts to make contact with Hally Chester over the past 30 years have met with failure.

Selected Filmography:

Crime School (1938, Boy)
Little Tough Guy (1938, Dopey)
Juvenile Court (1938, Timothy McGuire a.k.a. Lefty)
Personal Secretary (1938, Newsboy)
Little Tough in Society (1938, Murphy)
Newsboys' Home (1939, Murphy)
Code of the Streets (1939, Murphy)
Off the Record (1939, Reform School Inmate)
Call a Messenger (1939, Murph)
East Side Kids (1940, Fred "Dutch" Kuhn)
Boys of the City (1940, Buster)
Junior G-Men (1940, Murph)
Sea Raiders (1941, Swab)

Producer Credit Highlights

Joe Palooka film series (1946-51)
Models, Inc. (1952)
Night of the Demon (1957)
School for Scoundrels (1960)
The Secret War of Harry Frigg (1968)
Take a Girl Like You (1970)

TV Credits:

Take a Girl Like You (2000, Executive Producer)
School for Scoundrels (2006, Executive Producer)

Stanley Clements

Stanley Clements was born Stanislaw Kilmowicz, on July 16, 1926, on Long Island, New York, of Polish descent. When Stan was three years old, his mother, Anna, married building contractor Ignatius Adroncik. Along with his three older brothers (Benny, Joey, Walter) and two sisters (Anna Jr., Jennie), the family moved to Brooklyn.

Upon graduation from high school, where he picked up the nickname of Stash (Polish name for Stanley), Stan soon realized his true calling, as a performer. Stan danced and sang on the vaudeville circuit and after two years of hard work, it paid off. He was spotted by Major Bowes and signed to tour around the states as part of the Major Bowes Amateur Hour.

At the age fifteen, he was signed to a contract at 20th Century-Fox, appearing in his first film, *Accent on Love* (1941) with George Montgomery. Stan's second film, *Tall, Dark and Handsome* (1941), with Cesar Romero, saw him playing a tough-talking kid. Stan told a reporter in 1941 that he was confused by this role. "They didn't ask me to sing; they wanted me to be tough kid - not a singer."

Stan's career as an actor was confined mostly to appearing in small parts in such films as *Down in San Diego*, a loan out to MGM, and back at Fox for *I Wake Up Screaming*, starring Victor Mature, Betty Grable and Carole Landis.

In 1942 and '43 he was cast in three East Side Kids films for Monogram as one of the gang, but found roles in *The*

Photo of Stanley in the film *See My Lawyer*

45

Girl in the Case and, at Paramount, *Going My Way*. In the latter, he played the tough Tony Scaponi, leader of a bunch of kids who become friends with priest Bing Crosby. Again at Paramount, he was cast in *Salty Rourke*, as jockey Johnny Cates, receiving forth billing behind Alan Ladd, Gail Russell and William Demarest.

While serving in the Army (1944-1946), Stan wed starlet Gloria Grahame, in 1945; the marriage would end a few years later in 1948.

Stanley kept busy as an actor throughout the 1940s and '50s, appearing in over 40 films and 30 television shows.

In 1950 Stan met Maria Walek, actress Joyce Mackenzie's stand-in on the set of his film *Destination Murder*; a year later they wed, on December 17, 1951.

With the retirement of Leo Gorcey as the leader of the Bowery Boys in 1956, Clements took over for the last seven films made.

When the lights faded on the Bowery Boys in 1958, Stan once again turned his acting to the small screen, guesting on such shows as *Tales*

Publicity still of Clements from the film *Going My Way*

of Wells Fargo (1959), *Rawhide* (1960), *Wagon Train* (1963), *Daniel Boone* (1966), *Get Smart* (1969), *Gunsmoke* (1973), *The Blue Knight* (1975) and *Baretta* (1975). He also wrote the screenplay for the movie *Devil's Partner* (1962). Stanley's last film work came in the 1978 film *Hot Lead and Cold Feet* as a saloonkeeper.

In 1964, he and wife Maria adopted her eight-year-old nephew, Sylvester, from Poland, one of the first children adopted from behind the Iron Curtain. He and Maria divorced in 1974, but continued live together until 1979, when Stan was diagnosed with emphysema.

On October 16, 1981, the 55-year-old Stanley passed away from emphysema in Pasadena, California.

Author's Note:

Stanley and I became friends in the summer of 1970, when I wrote him a letter telling him that I was a big fan of his work in films. Our friendship lasted up till the day that he passed in 1981.

Stanley and I had many conversations (letter and phone) about his work with such actors like Alan Ladd, whom he did not care for, and Cesar Romero and Victor Mature, two of the nicest people he worked with. He told me how he was in love with Carole Landis, when the two worked together in *I Wake Up Screaming*. "Boy, she was pretty. She was a few years older than me; it was just puppy love on my end. We had a lot of fun playing cards. I think I won about $20 bucks from Mature and William Gargan. Not bad for being on the set only nine days."

We talked at great length about his son, Sylvester. He had been getting his feet wet in motion pictures by working in the technical side of the business.

When Stan and I met in person in March 1979, along with Billy Benedict and David Gorcey, at the Beverly Garland Hotel, Stan was somewhat frail due to his emphysema. He wore a fisherman's hat and his hair was grey, but he was all Stan.

The four of us had a great time during our visit. Benedict brought up the East Side Kids films, and Stan chimed in with his take: "It was pure chaos, but a whole lot of fuckin' fun!"

Stan and I talked with one another at least once a week. One day, in the fall of 1981, a package arrived in the mail. It was a plastic bag filled with yellow-orange powder, a powder mix for a new drink, which Stan and his friend, Gene Collins, had developed. It was similar to an Orange Julius.

A few weeks passed and, not hearing from Stan, I called his wife Maria. She told me that Stan was in the hospital; he had a short time to live. I called Stan at the hospital and he said to me, "Rich, buddy, I love you, too."

Selected Filmography:
  Tall, Dark and Handsome (1941, Detroit Harry Morrison, Jr.)
  I Wake Up Screaming (1941, Newsboy)
  'Neath Brooklyn Bridge (1942, Stash, an East Side Kid)
  Ghosts on the Loose (1943, Stash, an East Side Kid)
  Going My Way (1944, Tony Scaponi)
  See My Lawyer (1945, Willie)
  Salty O'Rourke (1945, Johnny Cates)
  Mr. Soft Touch (1949, Yonzi)
  Military Academy with That Tenth Avenue Gang (1950, Stash)
  Jet Job (1952, Joe Kovak)
  The Rocket Man (1954, Bob)
  Air Strike (1955, G.H. Alexander)
  Last of the Desperados (1955, Bert McGuire)
  Bowery Boys films (1956-1958, Stanislaus "Duke" Covelske)
  Sniper's Ridge (1961, Cpl. Pumphrey)
  Tammy and the Doctor (1963, Wally Day)
  It's a Mad Mad Mad Mad World (1963, Detective in squad room)
  Timber Tramps (1975, Joe)
  Hot Lead and Cold Feet (1978, Saloonkeeper)

TV Highlights:
  Broken Arrow (1958, Mingo)
  General Electric Theater (1960, Pete)
  Leave it to Beaver (1961, Shoe Salesman)
  77 Sunset Strip (1962, Red Jackson)
  Dr. Kildare (1964, Mr. Riccio)
  Perry Mason (1966, Floyd Walters)
  The Blue Knight (1975, TV Repairman)

Writer:
  Devil's Partner (1962)

Buddy Gorman

Born in New York, on September 2, 1921, Buddy grew up with dreams of becoming a professional baseball player. Buddy, a shortstop, was given a tryout for the Brooklyn Dodgers farm team, the Montreal Royals, at age 20. He was turned down because of his height (5'5").

Deciding to stay in California, he found employment at a flower shop. One day while making a delivery to the studios of United Artists, he was asked if he was there for work as an extra. He said yes, knowing that actors made more money than flower deliverers. (This story of how Buddy became an actor was told to me by Billy Benedict. How true it is, he did not know.)

Buddy appeared in 21 East Side Kid and Bowery Boy films, beginning with *Mr. Muggs Steps Out* (1943) and finishing up with *Let's Go Navy* (1951).

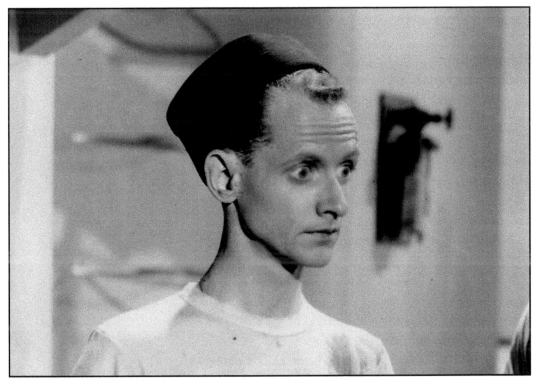

Buddy Gorman in a scene from *Let's Go Navy*

49

His other roles as an actor consisted of playing newsboys, telegram boys or messenger boys in films such as *Whistling in Brooklyn, The Very Thought of You* and *It's a Great Feeling.* He played a vendor at a drive-in the film *White Heat,* starring James Cagney. In my opinion, this was his best part.

After giving up acting in 1951, Buddy and his wife, Rosa Christoff, opened a novelty and magic store called Fun 'n Stuff in Los Angeles, California Buddy had been interested in magic from the time he was a small child. The store closed in 1995. Buddy's whereabouts are unknown.

Author Note:

On April 16th 2009 I found Buddy Gorman living in Webster New York.

He now lives at the Baywinde Senior Living Community, just outside of Rochester New York.

During my chats (April 16th, 2009 to present) with Buddy, I have come to know a few more things about him, that I did not know.

Such as his first name being Charles and that he has a daughter named Gretchen, and is the proud grandfather of Anika and Cally.

Buddy also told me that when he was an actor he used to be close friends with Orson Welles and Edgar Bergen. The three of them used to hang out frequently at a place called Hollywood Magic, where migicians practiced their craft.

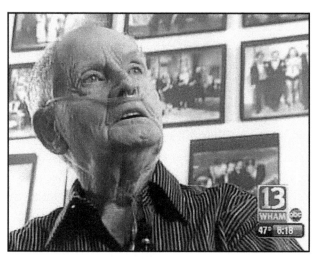

Recent photo of Buddy, taken April 16th 2009

At the time of this writing, two friends, Mendie Koenig and Buddy, who have not seen or spoken to one another in more than 40 years, have been reunited, and I have found my Holly Grayel.

Selected Filmography:

Hi Diddle Diddle (1943, Brokerage Firm Office Boy)
Whistling in Brooklyn (1943, Newsboy)
Higher and Higher (1943, Page Boy)
The Heavenly Body (1944, Newsboy)
And the Angels Sing (1944, Messenger)
Meet the People (1944, Youth)
Since You Went Away (1944, Private on Dance Floor)
I Love a Soldier (1944, Messenger)
Till We Meet Again (1944, Messenger)
The Very Thought of You (1944, Telegram Boy)
Meet Me in St. Louis (1944, A Clinton badger)
Thoroughbreds (1944, Roberts)
Roughly Speaking (1945, Florist shop boy)
It's a Pleasure! (1945, uncredited)
The Master Key (1945, chapter 3, Lug, boys' club member)
Meet Me on Broadway (1946, Golf caddy)
Cinderella Jones (1946, Sailor)

The Walls Came Tumbling Down (1946, Page Boy)
Night and Day (1946, English Page Boy)
Sing While You Dance (1946, Ralph)
The Jolson Story (1946, Jimmy, call-boy)
Wife Wanted (1946, Newsboy)
The Perils of Pauline (1947, Tomato thrower)
Key Witness (1947, Johnny)
Her Husband's Affairs (1947)
The Babe Ruth Story (1948, Copy Boy)
It's a Great Feeling (1949, Warner Brother's Studio, Messenger
White Heat (1949, Vendor at Drive-in)
The Reckless Moment (1949, Magazine Clerk)
A Modern Marriage (1950, Messenger Boy)

David Gorcey

With his black hair, good looks and sneer, David was destined to be an actor. The third son born to actor Bernard and Josephine, David was born on February 6, 1921, in Washington Heights, New York.

Following in his father's footsteps, he became an actor at the age of ten with his first part on the Broadway stage, in the play *Miracle at Verdun*, starring Edward Arnold. More stage work followed, including parts in the plays *The Good Earth* (1932) and *Dead End*, In the latter, he was first cast as a Second Avenue Boy, later taking over the role of Spit when older brother Leo went to Hollywood. David appeared in all 687 performances in the show's run.

Not too long after the play *The Good Earth* closed, he made his motion-picture debut in a *Penrod and Sam* 2-reel short, *The Detectives*, playing the part of Sam Williams, a part he would play four times. (This is where he met Bobby Jordan.)

Following older brother Leo to Hollywood in 1937, he was very busy, appearing with Gene Autry in *Prairie Moon*, *Sergeant Madden* with Wallace Beery, *City for Conquest* with James Cagney and *Tuxedo Junction* with Frankie Darro.

In 1938 he started his long association with The Dead End Kids in the Universal film *Little Tough Guy*. During filming, he was signed to a three-picture deal, along with Billy Benedict, Harris Berger, Hally Chester and Charles Duncan, for a series of films known as the *Little Tough Guys*, a splinter group of The Dead End Kids. With the success of these films, he was given a longer contract to appear alongside The Dead End Kids as a Little Tough Guy in such films as *Call a Messenger* and *You're Not So Tough*. At this time, the movie-going public

Photo of David Gorcey in the part of Sniper in *Little Tough Guy*

53

was a little confused; they could see David as an LTG in the DEK serial *Junior G-Men of the* Air and an East Side Kid at the same time. David had signed a film contract for Sam Katzman once his contract had ended with Universal, and the films were being released near the same time.

With the release of Monogram's second East Side Kid feature, *Boys of the City* (1940), David would now be known as one of the East Side Kids, playing the part of PeeWee in the next nine films.

From 1942 until 1945, David served in the U.S. Army as a medic overseas. Upon his release from active duty, he resumed his acting career with the film *The French Key* in 1946. That same year, he became one of The Bowery Boys, playing the role he is best remembered for, Chuck.

In the 1940s he wed a beautiful girl named Dorothea and in 1945 his son, David Jr., was born. By September of 1951, however, Dorothea had had enough of David's staying out all night and filed for divorce. This is when David changed his life around, stopped his drinking and became a reverend.

David would devote the rest of his life helping alcoholics and drug-addicted youths, opening a halfway house for them. David's grandson, David, told me that when his grandfather was running the Colonial halfway house, he would dress up as a doctor and sometimes get people who needed more serious help admitted to one of the big hospitals in Los Angeles. If he had not, they would have been turned away.

David remained with the series until its end in 1958. His film career, too, was coming to an end. He did some TV work in 1957 on Ed Sullivan's *Toast of the Town*, appearing as himself, and appeared on *M Squad*. His last screen work was that of a gunfighter in the film *Cole Younger, Gunfighter*, which starred Frank Lovejoy in 1958.

On October 13, 1984, David fell into a diabetic coma, and died on October 23, in Van Nuys, California. He was 63.

Author's Note:

In May of 1970, while I was talking to Stanley Clements on the phone, I mentioned to him that I was looking for David Gorcey. Stanley told me that he thought that David lived in Van Nuys, and if I found him I should pass along his number to him. The next day I did just that, as I found David's number and called him.

For the next fourteen years David and I were to become very close friends. We talked by phone at least once a week, sometimes more, depending on how big our phone bills were. We both did not like to write, but we sometimes did exchange letters.

Over the years we talked of his days as an actor and how he helped his brother, Leo, get a part in the play *Dead End*. He told me what he thought of all the kids and how he thought that Gabe Dell was the best actor in the whole bunch. He told me that he was a closet drinker, a recovering alcoholic, and that he had been sober for over twenty years.

We talked about the love he had for his son, David, and how he had prayed for his son's safe return from the Vietnam War. He was proud that his son was the first Gorcey to go to college, becoming something other than an actor. (David is a landscape architect for the city of Oxnard, California.)

We talked of him being a grandfather; David, born in 1978, makes his home in San Francisco and is in software, and Megan, born in 1982, is a teacher living in San Diego, recently married.

During one of our conversations, the subject of Stanley Clements came up. They had not talked or seen one another in about twelve years, and I put the two in touch together. Becoming pals once again helped Stanley, who had emphysema and was on oxygen. David helped him with his shopping, took him to doctor appointments, and even helped him pay some of his bills.

In March of 1979, I received a phone call from Huntz Hall's wife Lee wanting to know if I wanted to be a guest, along with Huntz and Gabe, on Tom Snyder's *The Tomorrow Show*, to meet them and talk about my hobby and the fan club that I had started on them. This was my chance to meet the guys I had only talked to by phone.

I called David and Stanley the same day and asked if we could get together once I was in California. We met that following Monday,

Gorcey in his last film, *Cole Younger Gunfighter* (1958), David Gorcey Jr., and grandson, David III

March 17. We met at the Beverly Garland Hotel at about 1:00 p.m. David told me that there would be a surprise waiting for me when I arrived.

When I arrived, I saw my surprise: David had called Billy Benedict and the four of us sat at a nice table way in the back so we could talk. For the next five hours, we talked of the days gone by, what it was like being an actor and about my hobby.

Billy told a story about the time Huntz and David were filming a fistfight on a Bowery Boy film, and how Huntz came out on the losing end. David said, "What fight? It was over in one minute." We talked about Judy Garland, James Cagney, Chester Morris (Boston Blackie) and about Donald Haines being killed in the war. We also talked about the worst directors and actors to work with, and the actors they liked the best. Billy preferred Cary Grant and Gloria Jean; Stan enjoyed working with Cesar Romero and Carole Landis, and David mentioned William Bendix and Laraine Day.

We took some pictures and exchanged a few photos. David gave me a photo of himself on the set of his last film (*Cole Younger*), Billy gave me his script from the Bowery Boy film *Jinx Money*, and Stan gave me two hats that he wore in films. One was from *Smart Alecks* (and looked like Leo's) and the other one from *Going My Way*. I didn't have much to give them, but I gave Billy a photo from the film *The Ox-Bow Incident*, Stanley the poster from *Salty O'Rourke* and David a limited-edition set of classical music records because he had told me that he loved this kind of music.

Before I knew it, our lunch had come to an end. We said our goodbyes and planned to stay in touch—and we did.

Selected Filmography:
  One Good Deed (1931, Sam Williams)
  Detectives (1932, Sam Williams)
  His Honor—Penrod (1932, Sam Williams)
  Hot Dog (1932, Sam Williams)
  Penrod's Bull Pen (1932, Sam Williams)

Juvenile Court (1938, Daniel 'Pighead' Olson)
Personal Secretary (1938, Newsboy)
Prairie Moon (1938, Hector 'Slick' Barton)
Off the Record (1939, Reform School Inmate)
Sergeant Madden (1939, Punchy)
City for Conquest (1940, First Ticket Taker)
Blues in the Night (1941, Jitterbug Dancer)
Tuxedo Junction (1941, uncredited)
Jail House Blues (1942, Bellboy)
The French Key (1946, Eddie Miller)
Killer McCoy (1947, Joe, Trainer Assistant)
The Babe Ruth Story (1948, Newsboy)
Wild Weed (1949, Ricky)
Abbott and Costello in the Foreign Legion (1950, Newsboy)
Cole Younger, Gunfighter (1958, Gunfighter with beard)

Stage Credits:

Miracle at Verdun (1931, Fritzchen)
The Good Earth (1932, Ensemble Cast Member)
Dead End (1935-1937, Second Avenue Boy and [1936- 1937] Spit)

TV Credits:

Toast of the Town (1957, Himself)
M Squad (1958, Desk Clerk)

Charles Duncan

The original Spit in the Broadway production of *Dead End* was born in Louisville, Kentucky, on March 12, 1920. In his senior year in high school he was the president of the drama club and was in three plays. At the end of the school year he set his sights on being a real actor and left for New York.

After knocking on doors for two months and getting nowhere, he landed the part of Spit in the play *Dead End*. He thought his future was set, but he was wrong. After only three months, his contract was bought out because he had come down with pneumonia.

On September 8, 1936, he was cast in the play *Bright Honor*, but the play folded after 17 performances.

Not finding work on the New York stage, he was off to Hollywood to try and cash in on being a Dead End Kid. Once there, he found an agent and was signed to a three-picture deal at Universal, who were about to start a series of films called the Little Tough Guys. By this time, Universal had been making films with the Dead End Kids.

After making the third and final film, he enlisted in the U.S. Air Force on February 23, 1940. Charles Duncan was killed in action as an air gunner in 1942; he had just turned 22 years old three months before.

In January of 1939 Duncan wed Ballet Dancer Gloria Newman. (Newman never remarried and passed away in 1997)

Author's Note:

When I talked to David Gorcey and Billy Benedict about Charles, they each told me that he was very bitter with the way things had turned out for him in the movie world. He thought he should have been one of the original Dead End Kids, not Leo.

Head shot of Duncan from *Little Tough Guys in Society* (1938)

They both told me that they had heard that Charles was killed while hitchhiking.

When I talked to Frankie Thomas about this, he said the circumstances surrounding Charles' death were untrue. Frankie said the real story is was that Charles was killed in action during World War II. "It was a shame that he never got a chance to reach his full potential; he was a very good actor," added Frankie. He also told me that Charles was a loner with a chip on his shoulder, but he did not know why. Frankie further revealed that Charles and Harris Berger were good friends and that, if he remembered correctly, the two of them bought a car together.

I received confirmation of Charles' death in World War II from the U. S. Air Force.

Filmography:
Little Tough Guys in Society (1938, Monk)
Newsboys' Home (1939, Monk)
Code of the Streets (1939, Monk)

Stage Credits:
Dead End (October 28, 1935 - January 3, 1936, Spit)
Bright Honor (September 1936 - October 1936, Cadet George [Red] Johnson)

Original caption: "A Matinee Idol with a cast iron chin, which belies his handsome good looks," 1938.

Harris Berger

Harris Franklin Berger was born on July 31, 1921, in New York City. His parents, Jacob and Mildred, had high hopes of Harris becoming a doctor, but their son had a different idea—acting. In October of 1935, at the age of fourteen, he had his first taste of acting in the play *Achilles Had a Heel* on Broadway. The play lasted for only eight performances, but Harris was now an actor.

In the spring of 1936, the play *Dead End* was in need of a replacement for Leo Gorcey as a Second Avenue Boy when Gorcey vacated the role for the part of Spit. Harris auditioned and was given the part. This role was to be short lived; Harris became a Dead End Kid, taking over the role of Dippy from Huntz Hall when the rights for the play were bought for the silver screen. He was also offered the part of Dippy in the

coast-to-coast tour of *Dead End*, with David Gorcey in the lead role of Spit. His dreams of being on the screen became a reality when the troupe reached Los Angeles.

Arriving in L.A. around the same time the film *Angels with Dirty Faces* was being shot, Harris answered a casting call for young actors. Along with actors George Offerman and Junior Coghlan, he was signed for the film, playing the basketball captain. This was also the start of his being tagged alongside The Dead End Kids.

A chance meeting on a bus with friend David Gorcey led to his becoming a Little Tough Guy. David was on his way to an audition at Universal Studios. With nothing better to do, Berger went along. With Gorcey, he was cast in the first film of the series, *Little Tough Guys in Society* (1938).

Harris would now be known as a Little Tough Guy and a member of The Dead End Kids. He would go on to appear in a total of four films and one serial with the group.

Publicity photo of Harris Berger from *Little Tough Guys in Society* (1938)

Before becoming an East Side Kid in 1940, he had parts in such films as *City for Conquest* and Oh *Johnny, How You Can Love.*

With the release of the Sam Katzman film *The East Side Kids* in 1940, he would reach his only fame, that as an East Side Kid, playing the part of Danny Dolan. He would appear in only one film away from the group, an uncredited role in *Private Buckaroo*, before he was drafted into the Army, where he remained until his discharge in 1945.

Trying to pick up his acting career where he left off was not to be. The only part he was cast in was that of a boy's club member in a spy serial, The Master Key (1945). Seeing the handwriting on the wall, he retired from acting.

Harris Berger passed away on November 21, 1983, from congestive heart failure, at the age of 62, in Simi Valley, California. His wife, Enid, passed away in 1990. His only son, Richard, is a sound technician for Sony Pictures.

Original caption: "It can't be done," when Harris announced his plans for becoming an actor, 1938

Author's Note:

I had been trying to find Harris Berger for about ten years. Billy Benedict, Frankie Thomas and David Gorcey told me that they had not seen or heard anything about him in over twenty years, and they had no idea where he might be. I had the initiative to call every Berger listed in the California phonebook; this would take some time because this entailed more than one hundred listed names. With high hopes, I made the calls.

I will never forget the date of June 3, 1982. I made a call to a clothing store that was called Bergers. It was about 2:30 in the afternoon; it was my 78th call. A lady by the name of Enid told me that her husband was indeed the Harris that I was looking for. He was out of the store at the moment; I should call back in about two hours.

I couldn't wait and I called an hour later. When the person on the other end answered, I knew it was him. I told him who I was, that I was a big fan of his and the Dead End Kids, and I asked if he could answer a few questions for me. He asked me if I could call him later, giving me his home phone number. That evening, I made the call, and we ended up talking for almost two hours.

Harris told me that after his time in the service, he had a tough time finding an acting job. He was no longer a teenager, and the studios weren't making kid films anymore. So, with the money he had saved, he opened his own clothing store in 1958 after working as a salesman for another store. He told me that he had not seen any of his acting friends in over 30 years and that the last person he did see was Billy Halop when they bumped into each other at an L.A. Hospital. Over the next hour or so, he told me that of all the people he worked with, James Cagney was the best.

He also told me that Huntz Hall and he were never friends, they were always at odds, and even had a fight at Jackie Cooper's house (Huntz lost). I asked him if he knew anything about Charles Duncan. He said that he and Charles were friends from their days in New York. I told him that Frankie Thomas told me that he and Duncan had bought a car together. "Yes, I think David Gorcey was in on it also," Harris told me. "The damn thing wouldn't go over 40 miles an hour. Hally Chester smashed it up; he hit a pole." I asked him about the story that Duncan had been killed while hitchhiking. "I don't know how that story about him ever got started," he told me.

I asked him if he got along with the other kids. "Well, Hally Chester and I were the best of friends; he and I would go out on a Friday or Saturday nights, with Judy Garland, Bonita Granville, Jackie Cooper, Frank Thomas, David Gorcey and sometimes with Jordan, Halop, Dell, Hall and Leo Gorcey. We would go dancing; we were both very good. I was a better dancer than Hally, but Leo and Hall were the best. I was friends with them all, but, like I said, Huntz and I weren't."

Before we hung up, I asked him if I could send him a few photos to autograph them for me. He told me that he had just been diagnosed with bladder cancer and that he was going into the hospital in two days, so the photos would take a few extra days getting back to me. He also said that he would look around for some stills to send me. He also told me that I was the best detective in the world, and that it was nice to be remembered.

About three weeks later, the autographed photos arrived, along with a two-page letter. The letter stated that the news on his health was not good; the cancer had spread and the doctors had given him a timeline of two years, at the most, on his life. Along with the letter, he sent me an 8x10 portrait from the film *Little Tough Guys in Society* that he autographed as well. The letter went on to say that he had a great time in films and met a lot of nice people in showbiz. He said it was nice to be remembered once again, that it was great medicine.

Over the next year we talked about seven or eight times by phone, sometimes for only a few minutes. The last time we talked was in October of 1983. I got the feeling from our conversation that his life was nearing its end.

On November 22, Harris' wife, Enid, called with bad news: Harris had passed away the night before from a heart attack. She thanked me for being such a friend. Harris had been touched by all of my letters and phone calls; it really meant a great deal to him that someone remembered him. Enid passed away in the fall of 1990.

Selected Filmography:
  Little Tough Guys in Society (1938, Sailor)
  Angels with Dirty Faces (1938, Basketball Captain)
  Newsboys' Home (1939, Sailor)
  Code of the Streets (1939, Sailor)
  Call a Messenger (1939, Sailor)
  Oh Johnny, How You Can Love (1940, Newsboy)
  City for Conquest (1940, Ticket Taker)
  East Side Kids (1940, Danny Dolan)

You're Not So Tough (1940, Jake)
Junior G-Men (1940, Sailor)
Give Us Wings (1940, Bud)
Mob Town (1941, Charlie, the paper boy)
Private Buckaroo (1942, Soldier)
The Master Key (1945, Boy's Club Member)

Stage Credits:
Achilles Had a Heel (1935, Ragamuffin)
Dead End (1936-37, Second Avenue Boy / Dippy)
Sunup to Sundown (1938, Ensemble Player)

David Durand

Known as a scene stealing actor, David was born David Parker Grey, on July 27, 1920, in Monroe, Michigan. When he was just an infant, his mother, writer-poet Odette, moved the two of them to California. David always told people that his father died when he was a year-old; in fact, his father died in Michigan in 1944 from a gunshot wound in a fight over money that was due him.

One day while he was roller skating in front of his house, film producer Hal Roach "happened by and saw me," David told the author. "He liked my smile and put me in two of the comedies, The *Sun Down Limited* and *Uncle Tom's Uncle*, and my film career began."

David acted non-stop in films for the next 18 years, working with Bette Davis in *Bad Sister*, *Viva Villa* with Wallace Beery, *The Life of Jimmy Dolan* (remade as *They Made Me a Criminal*), *Angels with Dirty Faces* with Cagney and the kids.

His first entry as an East Side Kid was the film *The East Side Kids*, done for Sam Katzman. He was not signed to a contract for this film; he wanted to remain independent and freelance. His scenes were later cut from the film.

When Bobby Jordan left the East Side Kids to enter the service, David, needing work, joined the cast as a full-time member. His last appearance as one of the gang was *Follow the Leader*. Prior to its release, in 1944, he was drafted into the Army and served as a signalman. His film career was over; it would be the last time he would be heard from until 1958.

Frank "Junior" Coghlan, who had worked with David in a few films, read a story in the *Chicago Tribune* that said that David was near

Shot of David Durand from the film *Naval Academy* (1941)

death from a bleeding ulcer and in need of a blood transfusion. The story stated that David was found in his own pool of blood and living on welfare.

Coghlan, stationed in Glenview, Illinois, in the U.S. Navy at the time, went to see his old friend. Frank supplied the blood that was needed, and all was well. This would not be the last time David made the papers.

Author's Note:

I met David in 1980 when I had come across an item in the *Chicago Sun-Times* saying that the former actor was looking for movie memorabilia. "Please contact the Green Tree Nursing Home," the ad read. Knowing this place was only ten

David signing a few photos with the author (July 1995)

minutes away from my home, I gathered some photos of David and was on my way.

David was not the same as I had seen him in his films; his muscular build was gone and most of his dark brown hair. However, his good looks still remained, as well as his smile. We talked for about three hours our first visit.

Over the next 18 years we had a standing dinner date at 5:00 p.m. every Wednesday. He would always sing the song "Louise," a song introduced in the film *Innocents of Paris* with Maurice Chevalier. We talked about his films and the actors that he worked with such as Bette Davis, Jackie Cooper, James Cagney, Frankie Darro, Junior Coghlan and, the love of his life, Anne Shirley—and, of course, the East Side Kids. They were not favorites of his.

In 1983 I became David's legal guardian. For him, this meant that I was to know where each and every dollar of his would be spent, as well as seeing about the kind of care he received. David had spent the remaining years of his life at the nursing home. He had sustained a head injury in 1973 which left him unable to care for himself.

David passed away, on July 25, 1998; two days shy of his 78th birthday. Frank Coghlan writes in his book, *They Still Call Me Junior: Autobiography of a Child Star,* that "David was a strange guy. He always seemed to be down on himself. I remember him being brought to the set by his crippled mother. Maybe this had something to do his paranoid attitude?"

Selected Filmography:

The Sun Down Limited (1924)
Uncle Tom's Uncle (1926)
Get Your Man (1927, Robert as a boy)
Tropic Madness (1928, Frankie)
Innocents of Paris (1929, Jo Jo)
Song of Love (1929, Buddy Gibson)
Ladies Love Brutes (1930, Joey Forziati)
Live and Learn (1930, Mike)
The Jazz Cinderella (1930, Danny Murray)
The Bad Sister (1931, Hedrick Madison)
The Spy (1931, Vanya)
Rich Man's Folly (1931, Brock Junior)
Probation (1932, David)
Forbidden Company (1932, Billy)
Silver Dollar (1932, Mark Martin)
The Great Jasper (1933, Andrew Horn)
Son of the Border (1933, Frankie Breen)
Jennie Gerhardt (1933, Willie Gerhardt)
The Life of Jimmy Dolan (1933, George)
As the Earth Turns (1934, Manuel)
Viva Villa (1934, Bugle boy)
Hat, Coat, and Glove (1934, Thomas Sullivan)
Wednesday's Child (1934, Charles "Chic" Nevins)
Little Men (1934, Nat Blake)
The Band Plays On (1934, Tony)
Wells Fargo (1937, Alex Trimball)
A Criminal is Born (1938, Rodney)
Off the Record (1939, Blackie)
Streets of New York (1939, Spike)
Boy's Reformatory (1939, Knuckles Malone)
Scouts to the Rescue (1939, Rip Rawson)
He Married His Wife (1940, Usher)
The Ghost Breakers (1940, Bellhop)
Golden Gloves (1940, Gumdrop Wilbur)
The Tulsa Kid (1940, Bob Wallace)
The Glove Slingers (Columbia Shorts, 1940-41, Terry Kelly)
Naval Academy (1941, Fred Bailey)

Radio:

Little Boy Blue (1922-1924)

Donald Haines

The freckled-faced Donald was born in New York in the summer of 1918. When he was ten, his father moved the family of four to California. His mother, a dancer in vaudeville, wanted Donald to be in show business, too. Being a typical stage mother, she was bound and determined to have her way.

Making the rounds of the studios, he was signed to a contract by Hal Roach for his Our Gang shorts. The first short Donald made was *Shivering Shakespeare* (1930); this was also the start of a great friendship between Donald and Jackie Cooper.

Donald made 15 more shorts films in the Our Gang series before he was cast in his first feature, *Skippy* (1931), starring Jackie Cooper This was followed by parts in such films as *No Greater Glory, A Tale of Two Cities, Little Lord Fauntleroy, Sergeant Madden* (with David Gorcey), *Boys Town*, and *Seventeen* (again with Cooper).

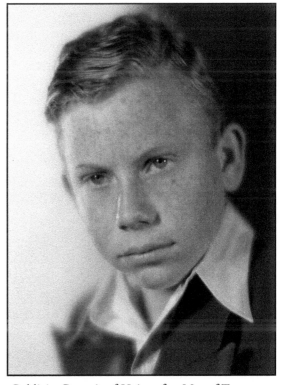

In 1940 he started his association with Sam Katzman and the East Side Kids, playing the part of Pee Wee in the first film, *The East Side Kids*. Donald went on to make a total of seven films as an East Side Kid.

On December 10, 1941, Donald enlisted in the U.S. Army Air Corps as an aviation cadet, reaching the rank of First Lieutenant. He was later killed in action, and he was listed as missing in action. His body was never found; there is no date of death, just the year 1942.

Publicity Portrait of Haines for *Men of Tomorrow*

Selected Filmography:
    Our Gang (1930-1934)
    Kidnapped (1938, Ransome, Cabin Boy)
    Boys Town (1938, Alabama)
    Never Say Die (1939, Julius)
    East Side Kids films (1940-1941, Skinny, PeeWee)
    Military training film (1941, Soldier, First Aid Demonstration)

Eugene Francis

Algy Wilkes, better known as Eugene Francis, was born on August 28, 1917, in Brooklyn, New York. At the age of 13, he made his first professional appearance on the New York stage for Eva Le Gallienne's production of *Peter Pan* in 1930. More Broadway plays followed, including *L'Aiglon*, with Le Gallienne and Ethel Barrymore; *Hamlet*, with Leslie Howard; *The American Way*, with Fredric March, his personal favorite; *Lady with Five Husbands* and *The Man Who Shot Lincoln*, which was done in the early part of 1940, the same year he went to Hollywood.

While having dinner one night at a friend's home, he received a call from his agent, Sue Carol, asking him to meet her at Sam Katzman's office for an audition. He got the part and was now an East Side Kid. Three more features followed as one of the gang.

In 1941 he was drafted into the Army and spent the next five years taking orders, once doing an army training film with Ronald Reagan at the Roach studios in 1943.

Upon his discharge in 1946, he was back on the East Coast resuming his career, finding work on radio and stage, doing such shows as *Lux Radio Theatre*, and voice-over commercials for Goodyear tires and Remington shavers.

During Gene's long career, in and out of show business, he was appointed television authority by the Actors Equity Association, and later became its national vice chair. Later, he was elected to the council of Actors Equity, elected to the Screen Actors Guild as their national vice president.

Shot of Gene in his days as an East Side Kid

69

In front of the camera, he appeared on *The Edge of Night, One Man's Family* and *As the World Turns.* He also wrote an episode for the George Sanders Show, "You Don't Live Here," and he was the host of his own radio show on Sunday afternoons on radio station WWDJ.

In 1985, he was the host and writer of the children's show *Calliope* on the USA network.

Gene, now 92, is now retired and lives in New Jersey with his wife. He is the proud father of Stephen, who makes his home in South Africa and is the creator and writer of Africa's most popular comic strip, *Madam & Eve*; he has two sons, Harrison, 18, and Carson, 15.

Eugene Francis, today

Author's Note:

I first made contact with Gene by letter in 1979 when I found his address in *Who's Who.* Over the years we have talked many times about his movie career and to this day he has no idea why the East Side Kids films are so popular. He is not a big fan of the films because of the low budgets.

Gene has told me a few things about his days as an East Side Kid, one of them about the film *Flying Wild*: "The cameras were rolling for a scene that was to have Leo Gorcey driving a Model T. Well, Leo went a little crazy behind the wheel and flipped the car over on its side: not wanting to waste film, the director, William West, let the shot stay in the picture." I asked Gene about Bobby Stone. He remembered Bobby as being "a little strange, very peculiar. He never looked like he knew what was going on, we weren't friends." As for Bobby Jordan and Leo, he said that he did not know them well, and that he only worked with them for about four weeks. "We just were not that close; my good friend was Donald Haines."

Selected Filmography:

Boys of the City (1940, Algernon "Algy" Wilkes)
That Gang of Mine (1940, Algernon "Algy" Wilkes)
Pride of the Bowery (1940, Algernon "Algy" Wilkes)
Flying Wild (1941, Algernon "Algy" Wilkes)
Army training film (1943, Private Eugene Francis)

Stage Credits:

Peter Pan (1930, Ensemble cast member)
L'Aiglon (1934, Acolyte)
Hamlet (1936, Page boy)
Glorious Morning (1938, Second Soldier)
The American Way (1939, Ensemble cast member)

Writer:

George Sanders Show (episode, "You Don't Live Here," 1957)

Frankie Burke

Frankie was born Francis Aiello, in Brooklyn, New York, on June 6, 1915. His father, Carmine, an immigrant from Italy, owned a small tailoring shop, and supported his family of seven, which included his wife, Marie, and their five children. Frankie worked in the tailor shop and sold newspapers to earn money to go to the movies to see his favorite actor, James Cagney.

Frankie was doing impersonations of Cagney, and was urged to go to Hollywood. Following this advice, he hopped a freight train to California. In Las Vegas, he briefly worked as a dishwasher to earn some money for expenses before actually arriving in Hollywood months earlier.

When he arrived in Hollywood, he decided to approach the actor to discuss their shared likeness, but the very busy Cagney was unreceptive. Frankie stayed in Los Angeles for awhile, hoping for another meeting, doing his Cagney impersonations on the Vaudeville circuit.

One evening a Warner Brothers talent scout was in the audience of a dinner club where Frankie was performing his act. The scout, usually not impressed by impersonators, was, nevertheless, impressed by Frankie's abilities.

However, Frankie, increasingly disenchanted with Hollywood and James Cagney, had decided to return to

Head shot of Frankie Burke for the film *You Can't Get Away with Murder* (1939)

Las Vegas, Nevada. In 1937, Frankie's boss at the Apache Hotel on the Las Vegas strip was reading a copy of *Variety* and read about a Warner Brothers casting call for a youth to portray James Cagney as a boy.

Underneath this ad was a notice taken out by Sol Baino, requesting the presence of the young Cagney impersonator he had seen on a certain date, in a certain club. Frankie was already entertaining the hotel guests with his impersonations, so his boss showed Frankie the *Variety* ad.

Frankie went back to Hollywood. When he arrived at Warner Brothers studios, the guard at the gate wasn't aware of the casting call and refused him access. Upset and fed up, he stuck out his thumb to hitch a ride back to the nearest train station. As luck would have it, Sol Baino pulled up to a stop light and saw Frankie. He picked up Frankie, took him to Warner Brothers, where Frankie was given a three-year contract along with the role of a young Cagney in *Angels with Dirty Faces*.

Frankie doing his best James Cagney, 1938

On October 27, 1940, Frankie married Frances Witherspoon, in Yuma, Arizona, three weeks after his fifteenth film was released (*The Quarterback*). In September of 1941, his only son, Richard, was born.

Sometime in late 1942 or early 1943, his marriage not working out, he took to the road again, boarding a bus to the East Coast, back to his family.

From 1948 through to the early 1960s, Frankie's life is a mystery. He claimed to have been a hobo the last twenty years of his life, hopping freight cars and living the carefree life.

In early March of 1983, he was taken from one of those boxcars by his fellow travelers to a nearest hospital in Chapman, Kansas, in grave condition. He was diagnosed with terminal lung cancer and placed in an intensive care facility called Chapman Valley Manor, where he languished until he passed away, at the age of 67, on April 7, 1983.

Though he appeared in only 18 films, he is best remembered for his portrayal of the young Rocky Sullivan in his first film, *Angels with Dirty Faces*, and his brilliant, dead-on impression of James Cagney.

Selected Filmography:

Angels with Dirty Faces (1938, Rocky, as a boy)
Off the Record (1939, Reform School Inmate)
Nancy Drew, Reporter (1939, Baggage Clerk)
The Adventures of Jane Arden (1939, Western)
You Can't Get Away with Murder (1939, Billard)
Women in the Wind (1939, Jonnie)
Sweepstakes Winner (1939, Chalky Williams)
Hell's Kitchen (1939, Soap)
Everybody's Hobby (C.C.C. Youth)
The Angels Wash Their Faces (1939, Reform School Inmate)
Pride of the Blue Grass (1939, Willie Hobson)
East Side Kids (1940, Skinny)
Fugitive from a Prison Camp (1940, Sobby Taylor)
The Quarterback (1940, 'Slats' Finney)
Ride, Kelly, Ride (1940, Skeeziks O'Day)
Model Wife (1941, Messenger Boy)
Shadow of the Thin Man (1941, Jockey Buddy Burns)

Billy Benedict

Billy Benedict was born in Haskell, Oklahoma, on April 16, 1917, and raised in Tulsa. Before becoming an actor, Billy sold newspapers, worked in a wheat field in Kansas and for a short time as a bank teller, being fired for not combing his hair, which was required of him. Billy, wanting to be a dancer, enrolled in a dance class, and was soon appearing in high-school plays, but after a few roles on the school stage he turned his attention to acting.

When Benedict was 17, he phoned 20th Century-Fox long distance and spoke to a casting director, who encouraged the young Bill to come to California. The seventeen-year-old William hitchhiked his way to Hollywood, with stops in Albuquerque and Las Vegas, where he found work as a dishwasher at a diner.

Portrait still of Benedict from the late 1930s

Once in California, he was given a film contract with the studio, due in part because of his persistence and nerve. His salary at the time of his first picture, *Ten Dollar Raise* (1935), was $75 dollars per week, a lot of money in those Depression days. Bill's services as an actor escalated and he soon found himself working with such stars as Janet Gaynor, Henry Fonda, Jean Harlow, Cary Grant and Katharine Hepburn. During the ensuing years, he worked with many of the major stars, Clark Gable, Spencer Tracy, Lucille Ball, Mae West, Irene Dunne and W.C. Fields, to name a few.

In 1938, Billy appeared in the Universal film *Young Fugitives*. This assignment led to him to being cast as one of the Little Tough

Guys in the *Little Tough Guys in Society*. This picture marked his long association with the Dead End Kids, Little Tough Guys, East Side Kids and Bowery Boys.

During the 1940s, Benedict was a busy actor in Hollywood, even making some serials, including *Adventures of Captain Marvel* (1941), *Perils of Nyoka* (1942), *Junior G-Men of the Air* (1942) and *Adventures of the Flying Cadets* (1943).

One of his best roles as an actor came in the film *The Ox-Bow Incident* (1943), in the part of a cowboy, working with friends Henry Fonda and Dana Andrews.

Benedict appeared in over 275 motion pictures and television shows, playing everything from Western Union messenger boys (Western Union paid tribute to Benedict by giving him his own official uniform) to a reverend on the TV show *Little House on the Prairie*.

Being a bachelor most of his life, he married a woman named Dolly in 1969. Ironically, they met during the filming of Barbra Streisand's *Hello, Dolly!*

Photo of Billy Benedict from 1998

After filming a segment for a TV film, *Bonanza: The Next Generation*, in 1988, Bill called an end to his acting career of more than 53 years and retired.

On November 2, 1999, Bill entered the hospital, suffering from a heart attack. Two days later, on November 25, Bill passed away from complications following heart surgery, at the age of 83. He is survived by his wife, Dolly.

Author's Note:

I had many conversations with Bill; a week wouldn't go by that we did not talk. Bill told me of his many hobbies, such as collecting hats. He told me of love of painting (oils), the cooking of breads, with recipes his mother taught him, and his love of square dancing ("I am not as good as I once was, I have slowed down a bit, but I like it"). He told me of his involvement with the Hillside Christian Church in Granada Hills, California, organizing fundraisers and food drives for the church, and his association with boys clubs and the YMCA.

In 1979 I had lunch with David Gorcey, Stanley Clements and Bill, a lunch which lasted for about four hours, with many stories told all around. One story which stands out was related by Bill: "One day while on the set, a fan approached me and asked, 'During a fight scene, how does your hat stay on?' I told him that I nail it to the back of my head, so that it doesn't come off. The guy said, 'Doesn't that hurt?' My reply was that, no, I have been doing it for years."

Selected Filmography:
Ten Dollar Raise (1935, Jimmy)
The Witness Chair (1936, Benny Ryan)
They Wanted to Marry (1937, Freckles
Tim Tyler's Luck (1937, Spud) (serial)
Little Tough Guys in Society (1938, Trouble)
Give Us Wings (1940, Link)
Adventures of Captain Marvel (1941, Whitey Murphy) (serial)
Junior G-Men (1942, Whitey) (serial)
The Glass Key (1942, Farr's receptionist)
Adventures of the Flying Cadets (1943, Cadet Zombie Parker) (serial)
Clancy Street Boys (1943, Butch, Cherry Street Gang Leader)
The Ox-Bow Incident (1943, Green)
Live Wires (1946, Whitey)
Crazy Over Horses (1951, Whitey)
Funny Girl (1968, Western Union Boy)
Hello, Dolly! (1969, News Vendor)

TV Credits:
Racket Squad (1951, Messenger)
Dragnet (1956-57, Himself)
Maverick (1958-59, Hotel Desk Clerk)
Ripcord (1962, Musician in Elevator)
The Twilight Zone (1964, Conklin)
Branded (1966, Hogan)
All in the Family (1971, Jimmy McNab)
Charlie's Angels (1976, Emmett Winston)
Little House on the Prairie (1981, Reverend Lyman)
Bonanza: The Next Generation (1988, Gus Morton)

Benjamin "Bennie" Bartlett

A red-headed, freckle-faced piano prodigy, Bennie Bartlett was born in Independence, Kansas, on August 16, 1924. By the time Bennie turned eight, he had composed over twenty compositions on the piano, which he played fluently. He also played the drums and trumpet.

In 1935, Bennie was in his first film, *Millions in the Air*, playing the piano. While filming the short *The Star Reporter in Hollywood* (1937), where he played one of his own compositions on the piano, Paramount signed him to a contract. He appeared in films with Fred MacMurray, Joan Bennett, Claire Trevor and Carole Lombard.

From 1935 until 1943, Bartlett worked in such films as *Sky Parade* (1936), *Maid of Salem* (1937), *Sons of the Legion* (1938), *The Family Next Door* (1939), and with Jackie Copper in the first Henry Aldrich film, *What a Life* (1939). Bennie played Butch Williams, the same name that was used when he later joined the cast as one of the Bowery Boys. (Cooper would be replaced by Jimmy Lyndon in the remaining films in the Henry Aldrich series.)

Bartlett was now freelancing as an actor, appearing in such films as *Men of Boys Town* (1941), *Meet John Doe* (1941) and *Code of the Outlaw* (1942), which led him to be cast in two East Side Kid features, *Kid Dynamite* and *Clancy Street Boys* (1943).

Publicity photo of Bartlett from his days as one of the Bowery Boys

In 1944, at the age of twenty, Bartlett joined the military, and for the next two years took orders from Uncle Sam.

Upon his discharge from the service in the spring of 1947, he was cast in two of the three Gas House Kids films (*Gas House Go West* and *Gas House Kids in Hollywood*), playing the part of Orvie. These two films paved the way for him to become a full-time member of the Bowery Boys, his first film being *Jinx Money* (1948). He was replacing Bobby Jordan, who had left the series in 1947.

Bartlett remained with the Bowery Boy film series until 1955, his last being *Dig That Uranium*. Before retiring at age 31, he appeared on two TV shows, *The Cisco Kid* (1953-1954) and *Combat Sergeant* (1956).

When Ben retired, he moved to Santa Barbara, California, where he became an insurance salesman. His only contact with show business was that of front man for his swing band. Bartlett and his six-piece band played all the swing spots in the California area.

Bennie Bartlett passed away on December 26, 1999, in Redding, California, at the age of 74.

Author's Note:

In my one conversation with Bennie Bartlett in 1985, he told me that it was fun being an actor and that he had met a lot of nice people, but he was now involved in the insurance field and happy doing it, no more rush-rush to get things done.

Selected Filmography:

Millions in the Air (1935, Kid Pianist)
The Texas Rangers (1936, David)
Penrod and His Twin Brother (1938, Chuck)
Just Around the Corner (1938, Milton Ramsby)
Let's Make Music (1941, Tommy)
Code of the Outlaw (1942, Tim Hardin)
Kid Dynamite (1943, Beanie Miller)
Gas House Kids in Hollywood (1947, Orvie)
Angels' Alley (1948, Harry "Jag" Harmon)
Hold That Baby (1949, Butch)
Cheaper by the Dozen (1950, Joe Scales)
Rear Window (1954, Man with Miss Torso)
Dig That Uranium (1955, Butch)

TV Credits:

The Cisco Kid (1953-54, Jimmy Winters, Matt Gray)
Combat Sergeant (1956, Himself)

Frankie Thomas

Frank Thomas was born on April 9, 1921, in New York. It was only natural that Frankie would become an actor like his parents, Frank M. Thomas and Mona Bruns. He grew up watching them perform on the New York stage. His parents encouraged him to give acting a chance, in the hopes that he might enjoy it; he did. In 1932, at the age of 11, he landed his first paying part as an actor in the play *Carry Nation* with James Stewart.

After appearing in the play *Wednesday's Child* in 1934, he made his debut in the screen version (with David Durand). More film work followed, as he appeared in the serial *Tim Tyler's Luck*, *Boys Town*, *Invisible Stripes* with George Raft and Leo Gorcey, and with the Dead End Kids *The Angels Wash Their Faces* and *On Dress Parade*.

In 1938, he was cast as one of the Little Tough Guys in *Little Tough Guys in Society*. He would make his last appearance with them as the gang leader in *Code of the Streets*, released in 1939. That same year he would team with Bonita Granville in four films in the *Nancy Drew* series.

Military duty called in 1942. He would serve in the U.S. Navy and the Coast Guard, before being discharged in 1947.

He moved back to New York, finding steady work on the radio and parts on early TV, in such shows as *Studio One* and the soap opera *A Woman to Remember*.

In 1950, Frank embarked on his favorite role, Tom Corbett, Space Cadet, on

Publicity photo of Thomas from the film *Flying Cadets* (1941)

television. Taking place 400 years in the future, Tom Corbett was a cadet in training for the elite solar guard. This 15-minute, five-day-a-week program helped make Corbett an all-American hero to children all over the U.S.

Not long after the end of the Tom Corbett series, Frank put away his makeup and retired from acting to teach Bridge, penning eleven books on the subject. This was his passion, and he taught Bridge all over the U.S., to sell-out crowds sometimes ranging in the thousands.

In 1980 he married Virginia, who had two children from a prior marriage. Virginia passed away in 1997.

On May 11, 2006, Frank passed away, from respiratory failure, in Los Angeles, California, at the age of 86. At his request, he was buried in his Tom Corbett, Space Cadet costume. He is survived by his children and a grandson.

Author's Note:

I first made contact with Frank in 1975 by phone and by mail after Frank Junior. Coghlan gave his number and address to me.

In 1979 I was able to have lunch with Frank and Junior at a restaurant in Sherman Oaks, California. Our friendship was to last some 31 years. It is hard to put 31 years of friendship and conversations into words, but I can share a few things.

We talked about films and the actors that he had met and worked with. We talked about Judy Garland and the boys that liked her, such as Bobby Jordan and Billy Halop, about politics and Ronald Reagan, and how he did not vote for him even though he was a friend. We talked about life and family, and how things have changed over the years. He told me how he called Buddy Gorman the "unhatched bird," because of his fuzzy hair, and the great times he had as an actor. We had many talks about Bridge and his friend Omar Sharif, who was an avid player of the game, on more than one occasion.

But, most of all, he was just my friend.

Selected Filmography:

Wednesday's Child (1934, Robert Phillips)
Tim Tyler's Luck (1937, Tim Tyler)
Boys Town (1938, Freddie Fuller)
Nancy Drew film series (1938-1939, Ted Nickerson)
One Foot in Heaven (1941, Hartzell Spence)
The Major and the Minor (1942, Cadet Clifford Osborne)

Stage Credits:

Carry Nation (1932, Kiowan Youth)
Little Ol' Boy (1933, Possum)
Thunder on the Left (1933, Martin)
Wednesday Child (1934, Bobby Phillips)
The First Legion (1935, Jimmie Magee)
Remember the Day (1936, Dewey Roberts)
Seen But Not Heard (1936, Duke Winthrop)
Your Loving Son (1941, Joshua Winslow, Jr.)

TV Credits:
A Woman to Remember (1949, Charley Anderson)
One Man's Family (1949, Cliff Barbour)
Tom Corbett, Space Cadet (1950-55, Tom Corbett)

Writing Credits:
Sherlock Holmes Bridge Detective (1973)
Sherlock Holmes Bridge Detective Returns (1975)
Sherlock Holmes and the Golden Bird (1979)
Sherlock Holmes and the Sacred Sword (1980)
Secret Cases of Sherlock Holmes (1984)
Sherlock Holmes and the Treasure Train (1985)
Sherlock Holmes and the Masquerade Murders (1986)
Sherlock Holmes and the Bizarre Alibis (1989)
Sherlock Holmes and the Panamanian Girls (2000)
Sherlock Holmes Mystery Tales (2001)
Secret Files of Sherlock Holmes (2002)

James McCallion

The one-picture Little Tough Guy was born on September 27, 1918, in Glasgow, Scotland. Sometime in 1928 his family immigrated to the United States, first coming to New York, where James's acting career began.

Jim's first part was that of a child in the play *Lysistrata,* at the 44th Street Theatre in 1930-31. It would run 252 performances. At the age of 18 he appeared on the New York stage for the last time in the play *Sea Dogs* (1939). That same year, he left for Hollywood.

Shortly after arriving, he landed a part in the RKO film *Boy Slaves,* which told the story of boy labor camps. At this time he made his only appearance as a Little Tough Guy, in *Code of the Streets,* the third and last film in The Little Tough Guy series. James made only one more film, *Pride of the Blue Grass* (with Frankie Burke), before entering the military.

By 1954 he was back on screen, in *Vera Cruz,* starring Gary Cooper and Burt Lancaster. His best role came in the 1963 film *PT 109,* which told the story of President John F. Kennedy's military service during World War II. James was singled out for his role as burn victim Pat McMahan in *Variety.*

Throughout the 1960s and '70s, James worked nonstop in films as well

Jimmy in a scene from *Pride of the Blue Grass* (1939)

as television, appearing in *Coogan's Bluff* with Clint Eastwood and TV shows like *The Big Valley* and *Mannix*.

In 1976, after an appearance on the show *The Blue Knight*, he decided that his career as an actor had come to an end, and he retired. Time was spent enjoying his woodworking and maybe some fishing.

James McCallion died of a heart attack, on July 11, 1991, in California.

Author's Note:

I first wrote to James in 1974, telling him that I was a big fan of his work in films and how much I enjoyed him in the film *Boy Slaves*. A few weeks later, I received an envelope in the mail. James had sent me a nice note thanking me for being a fan and a few 8x10 stills from the film. He also included his phone number. A friendship was started, with many letters and phone calls following.

James told me that Universal was to make a total of five Little Tough Guy films in all, with him being the leader in the last two, but that something happened with all of the kids' agents. He thought it was about more money.

He told me that David Gorcey and Billy Benedict were his close friends on and off the set. "We would all go to Jane Withers' house for parties or sometimes over to Jackie Cooper's home. There was always a crowd; from Frankie Thomas and his friends (Jackie Searl, Kenneth Howell, Tommy Kelly, Junior Coghlan and Bonita Granville) to Jackie's gang, which included Donald Haines, Jimmy Lydon, David Holt and Jimmy Butler, to Bobby Jordan and his cohorts, Wayne Morris, Edith Fellow, Judy Garland and, of course, Billy Halop, Huntz Hall, Gabe Dell and Leo Gorcey. Gorcey wasn't the way he was on screen; we got along just fine. We were all friends. We were always doing something, from going roller skating, to the movies and, when we had time, maybe a ballgame. We just had fun."

As Jim got older, our correspondence was less frequent; I think this was due to his wife Nora's death. But we still stayed in touch, just not as often, maybe four or six times a year.

In 2006, I was selling the film *Code of the Streets* on eBay. The winner turned out to be James' grandson. I sent him the DVD at no charge and have talked to him many times since.

Selected Filmography:
Boy Slaves (1939, Tim)
Pride of the Blue Grass (1939, Danny Lowman)
Code of the Streets (1939, Danny Shay)
Kiss Me Deadly (1955, Horace)
PT 109 (1963, Pat McMahon)

Stage Credits:
Lysistrata (1931, The Child)
But For the Grace of God (1937, Josey)
Roosty (1938, Roosty Nelson)
Sea Dogs (1939, Thomas)
Kathleen (1948, Christy Hanafey)

TV Credits (Highlights)

Four Star Playhouse (1955)
General Electric Theater (1956)
The Millionaire (1957)
Maverick (1958)
The Twilight Zone (1959)
The Untouchables (1960)
The Outer Limits (1963)
Wagon Train (1964)
Pistols 'n' Petticoats (1966)
The Andy Griffith Show (1967)
The F.B.I. (1970)
Mannix (1971)
Ironside (1974)
Barnaby Jones (1975)
The Streets of San Francisco (1976)
The Blue Knight (1976)

John Duncan

Good-looking tap dancer Johnny Duncan was born in Missouri, on a small farm just outside of Kansas City, on December 7, 1923. To make ends meet during the Depression, his father cut hair in the local barbershop on Saturdays. When he had free time from his chores on the farm, Johnny learned how to dance by going to the movies and imitating the stars on the screen. In 1938 he met a girl dancer named Lou Fischer and they formed an act called Duncan & Fischer.

While doing their dance act one night at the Tower Theatre in Kansas City, a talent scout from 20th Century-Fox was in the audience. The scout met with Johnny and his parents after the show and signed him to a six-month Fox contract. He was only 15 at the time.

After making his way to California with his parents, he made his acting debut in *Arizona Wildcat* (1939). His first brake as an actor came in the East Side Kid film *Clancy Street Boys*, as the rival gang member of the Cherry Streeters. His next film role came as a sailor in *Action in the North Atlantic*, with Humphrey Bogart; this was followed by the Frankie Darro film *The Gang's All Here*.

In 1943 he began his stint as an East Side Sid with *Million Dollar Kid*. When he wasn't making films, in his free time he could be found riding his Triumph motorcycle in the Hollywood Hills with the likes of Lee Marvin and Clark Gable.

Johnny Duncan, the rich kid, in the East Side Kids films

Johnny Duncan takes time to pose for a photo while recieving his Lifetime Achievement Award In Film From Blue Heron International Pictures. (Jan. 2009)

Johnny is best remembered on screen for his part as Robin in the serial *Batman and Robin* in 1949. After working on such TV shows, as *Dallas* and *Dynasty*, in the late 1970s and early 1980, he retired after more than 40 years in show business to his home state of Missouri. John has five children, ranging in age from 63 to 13.

Author's Note:

I met John and fellow actor Joe Turkel (*Angels in Disguise*) in 1993 at a Hollywood Collectable show in Chicago. We talked for about two hours that day and have remained good friends to this day.

Selected Filmography:

The Arizona Wildcat (1939, Town Boy)
Action in the North Atlantic (1943, Sailor)
Youth Aflame (1944, Jitterbug Dancer)
Batman and Robin (1949, Dick Grayson / Robin) (serial)

TV Credits:

Dallas (1978, Joe)
Dynasty (1981, Caretaker)

Ernest Frederick Morrison
(Sunshine Sammy)

Morrison was born in 1912, in New Orleans. Shortly after his birth, his father moved the family to California. Sammy became an actor by mistake. His father was a good friend of an owner of a movie studio, John Osborne, who was looking for a black baby for a film. The young Sammy did his part in the film very well and was soon working at Hal Roach studios.

He worked with Harold Lloyd and Snub Pollard at Roach. When Roach came up with the idea for the *Our Gang* series, the first person he cast for the series was Sammy.

After 28 *Our Gang* short films, Sammy left the series in 1924, for the vaudeville stage, where he would stay for the next 16 years.

When Sam Katzman began the East Side Kids films in 1940, he signed Morrison to appear alongside Bobby Jordan and Leo Gorcey for the second film in the series.

Leaving the East Side Kids behind in 1943, he was drafted into the Army. After two years of active duty, he was discharged in 1945.

Upon his release from the service, friend and agent Jan Grippo offered Sammy a part in his Bowery Boys films, but Sammy declined his offer. Instead, Morrison would spend the next 30 years working for a Los Angeles-based aircraft plant as an inspector.

After retiring to a life of leisure, the old acting bug came along, and Sammy came out of retirement. Starting in the 1970s, he appeared on such TV shows as *Good Times*, *The Jeffersons* and *227*.

Sammy Morrison passed away, on July 24, 1989, at the age of 77, in Lynwood, California.

Sammy Morrison

Selected Filmography:
  The Soul of a Child (1916, uncredited)
  Our Gang shorts (1920-1924)
  Gang War (1940, Gang Member)
  Fugitive from a Prison Camp (1940, Chuckles)
  The Ape Man (1943, Copyboy)
  Hit Parade of 1943 (Heaven Air Pilot)
  Greenwich Village (1944, One of the Four Step Brothers)

TV Credits:
  Good Times (1974, Messenger)
  The Jeffersons (1974, Friend of Family)
  Jim the World's Greatest (1976, Teacher)
  227 (1985, Garbage man)
  Passion and Memory (1986, Himself)
  American Masters: The Harold Lloyd Story (*The Third Genius*) (1989, Himself)

Bobby Stone

Bobby, born September 28, 1922, in Iowa, began his film career with a bit part in *Bringing Up Baby*, with Cary Grant and Katharine Hepburn, in 1938; he was 16 years old at the time. A few other parts followed in films, such as *Gangsters' Boy* and *Streets of New York*, both with Jackie Cooper.

In 1940 he was cast as Willie, one of the East Side Kids in the film *Pride of the Bowery*. During his stint as an East Side Kid, he would sometimes be one of the gang or, as in *Bowery Blitzkrieg* and *Mr. Wise Guy*, on the wrong side of the law.

Not wanting to be typecast as an East Side Kid, he found parts in such films as *Joan of Ozark, Secrets of the Underground*, and two serials, *The Secret Code* (1942) and *Hop Harrigan* (1946). His last film as an East Side Kid was *Follow the Leader* in 1944.

Bobby resurfaced as an actor in the Elvis Presley film *Kissin' Cousins* (1964). That same year, he teamed up with Sam Katzman. At Four-Leaf Productions Bobby was a unit production manager on all of Sam's films, including *Harum Scarum, Your Cheatin' Heart* and *A Time to Sing*.

In early 1970 he was the associate producer for the film *How to Succeed with Sex*.

Bob passed on May 9, 1977, from cancer, at the age of 55, in Los Angeles, California, leaving behind a son, David, and daughter, Sandra.

Author's Note:
In the fall of 1976, I was able to make contact with Bob, who at the time was suffering from cancer. Our phone calls to one another would last for about 10 or 15 minutes each, at the most, but he was kind enough to send me a few autographed stills from some of the different films he was in.

Bobby Stone as one of the East Side Kids

He told me that he had fun doing the East Side Kids pictures. He said that he was good friends with Gabe and Sammy, but had not seen them in a few years. Of all the films that he was in, the serial *Hop Harrigan* was his favorite and that Elvis Presley was the most down-to-earth person that he worked with.

At the time of his death, he was busy writing a screenplay for Warner Brothers.

Bobby & Elvis Presley share a moment on the set while filming *Harum Scarum* (1965)

Selected Filmography:
> *Gangster's Boy* (1938, Salvatore)
> *Bringing Up Baby* (1938, Bit part)
> *Streets of New York* (1939, Beansy)
> *Gangster's Boy* (1938, Salvatore)
> *Down Argentine Way* (1940, Panchito)
> *Pride of the Bowery* (1940, Willie)
> *East Side Kids* films (1940-44, Monk Martin, Chalky Jones, Skinny, Speed, Rocky)
> *Hop Harrigan* (1946, Gray) (serial)
> *I, Jane Doe* (1948, Newsboy)
> *Train to Alcatraz* (1948, Hollister)
> *Kissin' Cousins* (1964, General's Aide)

Production Manager:
> *Angel, Angel, Down We Go* (1969)
> *A Time to Sing* (1968)
> *For Singles Only* (1968)
> *The Fastest Guitar Alive* (1967)
> *The Love-Ins* (1967)
> *Riot on Sunset Strip* (1967)
> *Hot Rods to Hell* (1967)
> *Hold On* (1966)
> *Harum Scarum* (1965)
> *When the Boys Meet the Girls* (1965)
> *Your Cheatin' Heart* (1964)
> *Get Yourself a College Girl* (1964)

Producer:
> *How to Succeed with Sex* (1970)

Norman Abbott

The one-time Dead End Kid was born in New York City. At the urging of his mother, stage and vaudeville actress Olive Victoria, he made his way to Hollywood in 1941.

Upon arriving in California, Abbott's uncle, Bud Abbott, found him employment as his stand-in on the films *Who Done It?* (1942) and *Hit the Ice* (1943).

With his foot in the door at Universal, where both films were made, he was cast in the last Dead End Kid film, *Keep 'em Slugging* (1943), in the role of Ape, a character originally played by Bernard Punsly.

Abbott's career as an actor came to an end when he was drafted into the Army in 1943.

Upon his discharge, he picked up where he left off, but this time as dialogue director for two Abbott & Costello films, *The Wistful Widow of Wagon Gap* (1947) and *Africa Screams* (1949). He also married around this time, to Jane Woodward.

Abbott began branching out from being a dialogue director to directing actors, on such TV programs as *Bachelor Father* (1959-60), *Leave it to Beaver* (1960-62), *McHale's Navy* (1963), *The Jack Benny Show* (1964), *The Munsters* (1964-65), *Get Smart* (1967), *The Brady Bunch* (1970), *The Ghost Busters* (1975), with friend Huntz Hall, and *Welcome Back, Kotter* (1978-79).

In 2003 he was interviewed on the TV show *Biography: The Munsters: America's First Family of Fright*, along with the cast he directed on the show, Yvonne De Carlo, Butch Patrick and Al Lewis.

At the time of this writing, he is still going strong, but is now retired, and has left the show-business part of his life to son William (Bill), who has been a music editor on such films as *Das Boot* (1981), *Legends of the Fall* (1994), *Men in Black* (2002), *Spider-Man 2* (2004) *Charlotte's Web* (2006), *Meet the Robinsons* (2007), and *Lions for Lambs* (2007).

Norman Abbott

Jordan, Abbott, Hall, Dell and Shemp Howard in a scene from *Keep 'Em Slugging*

Author's Note:

In my two conversations (1985) with Mr. Abbott, he told me that he liked being known as one of the Dead End Kids, but that most people don't remember him ever being an actor, let alone a Dead End Kid. He sent me a few autographed pictures from his only film as a Dead End Kid, and a few others from films he had done, and wished me luck.

Filmography:

Grand Central Murder (1942, Whistling Messenger)
Whistling in Dixie (1942, Attendant)
Keep 'Em Slugging (1943, Ape)
The Wistful Widow of Wagon Gap (1947, Dialogue Director)
Africa Screams (1949, Dialogue Director)
Katie Did It (1951, Chick)
Walking My Baby Back Home (1953, Doc)

TV Director Highlights:

Bachelor Father (1960)
Leave it to Beaver (1960-62)
McHale's Navy (1963)
The Jack Benny Program (1964)
The Munsters (1964-65)
Get Smart (1967)
The Brady Bunch (1970)
Sanford and Son (1974-76)
Welcome Back, Kotter (1978-79)
The Munsters Today (1988)
Pop-Up Brady (2001)

Eddie LeRoy

New York-born Ed began his career as a performer in 1947, at the age of 14, singing and dancing in nightclubs. Being underage at the time, he had to be sneaked into each club. Playing in such cities as New York, London and Las Vegas, he headlined at the Flamingo Hotel for eight weeks.

Branching out to motion pictures in 1948, his first role was *The Vicious Circle*, followed by *The Happy Years*.

He was signed to play Ben Whitledge in *The United States Steel Hour's* live TV production of *No Time for Sergeants* in 1956. This same year he became known to fans as one of the Bowery Boys, Blinky. It was a part he would play until the series ended.

Moving back to television in the early 1960s, he was a frequent guest star on such shows as *The Red Skelton Show* and Milton Berle's show. He was also the on-air TV spokesman for 7UP for more than twenty years (1960-1983).

He is currently working behind the scenes as a producer and director for Sonny Fox Productions and has no plans of retiring. Ed resides in Burbank, California, and has just celebrated his 74th birthday.

Photo of Eddie Le Roy endorsing 7UP

Author's Note:

I had the great pleasure to meet Eddie when I was in California in March of 1979. We met at a place called The Farmers' Market in Burbank. Once we started talking, we couldn't stop. He thanked me for being such a loyal fan with my letters over the years and asked me if I would send him a copy of Leo's book if I was to come across one.

We talked about our dear friend Stanley and the fact that he was not well. Our morning breakfast coming to an end, and as we were saying our goodbyes, he asked if I had Stan's address and phone number with me, and I gave it to him.

On October 28, 1981, I received a letter from Ed that said the following:

Dear Dick,

Please excuse me for taking so long to answer your last letter of condolence regarding our very good friend, Stanley. Stanley was one of the "rare" people in our industry: kind, generous, and caring! I spent many long days and nights with him at "the end."

Stanley spoke many times about you, your collection...and mostly, your friendship - which he valued very much.

Thank you for all of the movie material that you have been sending on me. Gee, I wish that I had something to send you.

Till the next time we talk. Let's say a prayer for Stan.

Your Bowery Boy friend - Eddie (from now on please call me Eddie)

Over the years we have corresponded with each other quite regularly. Eddie is a dear friend.

Selected Filmography:
   Mickey (1948, Bit Part)
   The Vicious Circle (1948, Samuel Schwartz)
   The Happy Years (1950, Poler Beekstein)
   Bowery Boys films (1957-58, Blinky)

TV Credits:
   The United States Steel Hour ("No Time for Sergeants," 1955, Ben Whitledge)
   Born and Bred (1978, Lounge Singer)

William (Bill) Lawrence

Bill Lawrence was born on December 28, 1926, in Joliet, Illinois, a small town just outside of Chicago, where his father had a farm. In the winter of 1936 his family moved to California.

I met Bill by chance in 1976, when I read a newspaper article about a place called the Inn that was once owned by former gangster Al Capone. The Inn, the article went on to say, was now a restaurant and was located in Joliet and up for sale. I decided to take a drive to check the place out. When I finally found the place, I was greeted by a man who was the janitor who said I could look around. I told him that the place looked like an old "B" movie set. Our conversation kept coming back to old movies, when he told me that he was once an actor and worked with Leo Gorcey. He took me to a room at the back of the building, this was now his home. Once inside the small, 12x12, space, I saw about 20 picture frames on the walls; they were of him when he was much younger. They were photos when he had appeared on Ed Sullivan's *Toast of the Town, The Arthur Godfrey Show* and him with Leo Gorcey. Now, he looked familiar,

now knew who he was: Bill Lawrence, a former East Side Kid, from *Mr. Wise Guy*. I had to ask him why he was no longer an actor in films. He told me that he had a drinking problem which had ended his days in

Hollywood. I saw Bill at least every month for the next two years. We talked about his days as an actor, watched some of his films on VHS tapes.

Bill passed away on October 12, 1978, at Silver Cross Hospital, in Joliet, Illinois, from liver failure. He was 51. Bill once told me an empty bottle of booze is like an empty life: "What's the point?"

Sam and Jack Edwards

Brothers Sam and Jack grew up in a show-business family, having both made their stage debuts as babies in the play *Tess of the Storm Country* their mother, Edna Park, in 1917.

The brothers were born in Macon Georgia. Sam, being the older brother of the two, was born on May 26, 1915; Jack followed a year later, in April.

They appeared together on the radio show *The Adventures of Sonny and Buddy*, in which they played boys who run away to join a traveling medicine show, and on their family's show, *The Edwards Family*.

Jack started his film career first, having a small part in the silent film *I Do* (1921), billed as Jackie Edwards. This was followed many years later by his part as Algernon Mouse Wilkes in the first East Side Kids film. He was last seen on screen in Bob Hope's *The Ghost Breakers* (1940), along with fellow East Side Kid David Durand

After being drafted in 1941, he served two years and was discharged in 1944.

Jack left acting behind to go into radio, where he stayed for the next 50 years. He is now retired and living in California.

Sam's one and only appearance as an East Side Kid was that of Pete. He was drafted into the Army shortly after the film's release and his East Side Kid days were over. During his three-year hitch, he

Sam Edwards as Pete.

entertained the troops in Africa, Italy and Asia, before being discharged in 1945.

After returning from military service, he resumed his acting career in such films as *The Street with No Name* and *Twelve O'Clock High* as Lt. Birdwell.

Moving to television in the 1950s and '60s, Sam worked regularly, appearing on such shows as *I Love Lucy, Hazel, The Andy Griffith Show* and *Mission: Impossible*. He was also was heard in the cartoon classics *The Flintstones* and *Jonny Quest* and voiced the characters of Owl and Tigger on *Winnie the Pooh* records.

Sam's last role as an actor was in a recurring part on TV's *Little House on the Prairie*. He retired from acting in 1978, moving to Durango, Colorado.

On July 28, 2004, Sam passed away, at the age of 89, from a heart attack.

Author's Note:

I wrote a letter to Sam in 1980 telling him that I was a big fan of the East Side Kids, asking him if he would be

Jack Edwards as Algernon "Mouse" Wilkes

kind enough to autograph a couple of pictures for me. He did, and along with the photos he sent me his brother Jack's address as well. I kept in contact with Sam until his death in 2004.

Jack sent me a few autographed stills and a short note saying that he had fun doing the East Side Kid picture, but that part of his life was now over and he did not know about the other actors that he worked with.

Mickey Martin & Wesley Giraud
Second Avenue Boys

Mickey Martin was born in Arizona, on November 16, 1920. Before his role in the film *Dead End*, he appeared in such films as *The Throwback* (1935) and *It Could Happen to You* (1937). Besides working with the Dead End Kids, he also worked with Bobby Jordan in the film *Reformatory* and with Leo Gorcey in *Gallant Sons*. During his film career, he worked with Orson Welles in *Citizen Kane*, Mickey Rooney in *Killer McCoy* and with Dana Andrews in *While the City Sleeps*.

In the late 1960s he moved from films to television, appearing on such shows as *The Ed Wynn Show* and *December Bride*.

His last role came in 1967, that of a bellboy, in the film *The Gnome-Mobile*. The tough kid, with the mark of the squealer, passed away on July 25, 1973, of a heart attack, in Los Angeles, California.

By the time Wesley Giraud appeared in the film *Dead End*, as one of the Second Avenue Boys, he was already a seasoned performer of more than sixteen films. Coming to California from New York in 1932, at the age of 13, he was cast in his first film, *One Man Law*. Other film roles followed, working with the likes of Gary Cooper in *The Plainsman* and with Spencer Tracy in *Boys Town*. Wesley's last screen role came in *Gallant Sons* in 1940, which also featured Leo Gorcey.

On January 30, 1941, Giraud enlisted in the U.S. Army for a period of four years. Upon his discharge, in 1945, he went to work for the U.S. Postal Service as a letter carrier in Santa Monica, California.

Second Avenue Boys Wesley Giraud and Mickey Martin and Billy Halop, in a scene from *Dead End*

In 1972, at the age of 54, Giraud suffered a stroke that left him with speech difficulty. On May 3, 1993, at the age of 74, Wesley suffered a massive stroke at his home in San Diego, California; he died two days later, on May 5.

Author's Note:

Martin and Giraud were the perfect actors to play the parts of The Second Avenue Boys. They should not be overlooked, as they were both essential to the film *Dead End* as the rival gang members.

Supporting Players

**Charles Peck, Ronald Sinclair, Ward Wood,
Kenneth Howell, George Offerman, Jackie Searl,
Gil Stratton, William Tracy**

Charles Peck

Playing the rich kid Philip Griswald, the film *Dead End* was the start of Peck's long career in show business. Peck was born on December 19, 1922, in New York City, and moved to California in 1935 with his mother.

With only a few minor credits in radio under his belt, he landed the part of the spoiled brace-wearing rich kid in *Dead End*.

In 1939, he appeared in a series of films called The Peppers, playing the part of Ben Pepper. The four-film series were similar to the Henry Aldrich and Andy Hardy films.

Other films he appeared in were *Judge Hardy's Children*, *The Adventures of Mark Twain*, *A Christmas Carol* (along with Ronald Sinclair, who would work with The Dead End Kids in *They Made Me a Criminal*), and *Boy Slaves* (along with Little Tough Guy James McCallion). In the latter film, Charles played his familiar role of the snobby rich kid.

Taking a break from acting in the 1950s, he became a sound mixer for films and TV. Among his credits are *An Affair to Remember*, *The Gift of Love* and *Rawhide*.

By the late 1970s the acting bug began to bite again, and he guest starred on such TV shows as *Hawaii Five-O* and *Magnum, P.I.*

Peck passed away in the fall of 1999, in California.

Author's Note:

I wrote a letter to Charles in 1983 when he was a guest star on the TV show *Magnum, P.I.* In my letter I asked if he would please autograph a picture for me and if he could tell me anything about working with the kids. His reply was nice; he autographed the photo, and said that he had fun hanging out with the kids. He also stated that his son, Charles, was a writer and producer, mainly for the stage.

Publicity photo of Charles Peck, from the film *Dead End* (1937)

Ronald Sinclair

Sinclair was born Richard Arthur Hould, on January 21, 1924, in Dunedin, New Zealand. Emigrating to the U.S. in 1930, he first went to New York before settling in California in 1935.

His film career began in 1936, at the age of 12, when he was cast in the film *Beloved Enemy*. During the 1930s and '40s he was in such films as *Boots and Saddles, Dangerous Holiday, Thoroughbreds Don't Cry* (with Mickey Rooney) and *They Made Me a Criminal*.

Sinclair wore many hats in the film industry, such as producer, editorial director, sound engineer and music director. He returned to acting for the last time in 1967 with the film *The Big Catch*.

In 1988 and 1990 he was the sound director for the Bruce Willis films *Die Hard* and *Die Hard 2*. He then retired.

Sinclair passed away, from respiratory failure, on November 22, 1992, in Woodland Hills, California, at the age of 72, leaving a wife, Carol, and a son.

Author's Note:

I was able to make contact with Sinclair by mail in 1987, at the time he was working on the film *Die Hard*. He sent me an autographed picture and wished me well; he could not shed any light on working with the Dead End Kids except to say they were a very rowdy bunch.

Photo of Ronald Sinclair, when he was known as
Richard Arthur Hould

Ward Wood

Ward was born on April 8, 1924, in California. In 1943, at age 19, he made his first film, *Adventures of the Flying Cadets*, being billed fourth behind Johnny Downs, Bobby Jordan and Billy Benedict. This same year he also worked with John Garfield in the film *Air Force*.

In the early 1950s he turned to acting on the small screen, doing such shows as *The Cisco Kid, Space Patrol, M Squad* and *Have Gun - Will Travel*. During the 1960s and '70s he branched out as a writer and producer on shows like *The Rifleman* and *The Blue Knight*.

Ward Wood is probably best remembered for his role of Lt. Art Malcolm on the TV show *Mannix*, which ran for seven years (1968-1975).

Before retiring in 1983, he had one last role, playing a doctor on a CBS Afternoon Playhouse Special.

Ward Wood died on November 3, 2001, in Santa Monica, California, at the age of 72.

Author's Note:

I wrote a letter to Ward in 1976 asking him for an autographed photo and telling him how much I enjoyed his work with Billy Benedict and Bobby Jordan in *Adventures of the Flying Cadets*. About six months later, I received my photo and short note that read, "While making the film with Jordan, Benedict and Johnny Downs, we all went to an Air Force Base and entertained the troops. Here is a picture from that day. Thanks for your kind words."

Ward Wood in a scene from the serial *Adventures of the Flying Cadets*

Kenneth Howell

Howell was born in Los Angeles, California, on February 21, 1913. Kenneth wanting to be an actor and, with his mother's support, he enrolled in dance and acting classes. By the time 1935 arrived, he was a seasoned performer of fourteen films.

His big break came in 1936, when he signed a contract with Twentieth Century-Fox to appear as the oldest son in the Jones Family pictures. From 1936 to 1940, sixteen Jones Family films were made. While under contract, his services were loaned out for other films, such as *A Star is Born* and *The Little Red Schoolhouse*.

In 1940 he worked alongside the Dead End Kids in the film *Junior G-Men* and the East Side Kids feature *Pride of the Bowery*.

At the outbreak of World War II, he enlisted in the U.S. Navy in the Medical Corp. Before being shipped overseas, he married long-time girlfriend, Marguerite A. Thomson (1942). On September 9, 1943, his only child, Stephanie Rye, was born. After being married for three years, his marriage ended in divorce with the realization that he was gay. Kenneth never had contact with his daughter from the age of five until she turned 21, when she called him on the phone; they never met.

Howell's last screen role was in *In Old Amarillo* (1951). Howell committed suicide on September 28, 1966, in Long Beach, California.

Publicity shot of Kenneth Howell

George Offerman, Jr.

Offerman was born in Chicago on March 14, 1917, when his parents, George and Marie, were doing a play in the windy city. Wanting to follow in his parents' footsteps, he became an actor. His first role was on the New York stage in *The Little Poor Man* (1925). Venturing into films in 1927 (*The Broadway Drifter*), he would continue to act on screen for the next 32 years. He worked with many of the actors of the day, such as Cagney, Bogart, Garfield, Cooper and Van Johnson. His best role as an actor came in 1944 as Joe Sullivan in *The Fighting Sullivans*, which told the true story of the five Sullivan Brothers killed in action during World War II. During the 1950s he was on TV shows such as *Dragnet, The Cisco Kid* and *Bat Masterson*.

George made the first of many appearances with the Dead End Kids in the 1938 film *Crime School*, as Red, the reform school "old-timer." Although he was never part of the group, he appeared in eight of their films, the last one being *Let's Go Navy* (1951), a Bowery Boy comedy.

While living in New York, doing rehearsals for a play, he passed away at his home on January 14, 1963, of a heart attack.

George Offerman Jr. as Red in
Crime School (1938)

Jackie Searl

John E. Searl was born on July 7, 1920, in California. At the age of eight, he was on screen for the first time in the film *Daughters of Desire*. Other films followed, such as *Tom Sawyer, Skippy* and *Huckleberry Finn*.

Known as a bratty kid on films, he was the perfect counterpart to Jane Withers.

Not satisfied with the brat roles that were coming his way, though, he began seeking more adult-oriented roles.

His first one was the Universal film *Little Tough Guy*, which starred the Dead End Kids. He would appear with the kids in two more films, *Little Tough Guys in Society* and *The Angels Wash Their Faces*. He also worked with Bobby Jordan in *Military Academy*.

Jackie joined the military in 1942. Upon his discharge in 1946, he tried to resurrect his career, but he had a tough time in the movie world and turned to television.

He appeared on such shows as *Lassie, Gunslinger, Perry Mason, Gunsmoke* and *Bonanza*.

Jackie retired in the 1970s to his home in Tujunga, California. He died on April 29, 1991, at age 70.

Author's Note:
One day while Frank Coghlan and I were talking on the phone, I mentioned

Scene from Little Tough Guys "In Society," a Universal production. printed in U.S.A.

The Little Tough Guys (L to R), Frankie Thomas, Harris Berger, David Gorcey, Charles Duncan, Searl, Billy Benedict and Hally Chester.

that I was looking for Searl. Frank said he would call me back in a few days if he could turn something up. A couple of days later Frank called; he had found an address for me.

I wrote Jack a short letter telling him that I was a big fan and enclosed a photo for him to sign. About a month later, I received my autographed photo and a very short note, saying, "What was then is the past and should stay that way. Please feel free not to write me! Thank You."

Gil Stratton, Jr.

Gil was born June 2, 1922, in Brooklyn New York. The two-time Bowery Boy got his start on the Broadway stage in the musical play *Best Foot Forward* in 1941, playing the part of Bud Hooper. Following the success of the play, he was summoned to Hollywood, but was instead given a part in *Girl Crazy*; his role in the screen version of *Best Foot Forward* was filled by Tommy Dix. Gil appeared in such films as *Dangerous Years* (1947), *Stalag 17* (1953) and *The Wild One* (1953) as one of Marlon Brando's motorcycle gang members.

In 1954 Gil embarked on a new career, as a sportscaster for the CBS television station KNXT in Los Angeles, where he did the play-by-play for the L.A. Kings hockey team. Gil would make only two more films, *Sextette* (1978) and *Dismembered* (2003). Gil retired from the station in 1984, with twenty years of service, retiring with his wife to Hawaii, while retaining a home in Toluca Lake, California.

Gil Stratton passed away on October 13, 2008, at his home in Toluca Lake, at the age of 86. He is survived by his wife, Dee (Arlen), of 47 years and his five children, Gilda Stratton, Billy Norvas, Gibby Stratton, Laurie O'Brien, and Cathy Stratton.

William Tracy

The Pittsburgh-born Tracy was born on December 1, 1917. He got his start on the Broadway stage with a small part as a delivery boy in *Hitch Your Wagon* in 1937. This was followed by the play *Brother Rat* (1937), in the role of Misto Bottome, which saw him the following year reprising his role in the screen version.

When a casting call went out for the film *Angels with Dirty Faces* for actors looking like a young Pat O'Brien, it was Pat's father who discovered the young actor to play his son as a boy on screen. The young Tracy had been seen in the film *Brother Rat* by O'Brien's father.

Tracy also had roles in such films as *Gallant Sons*, *Tobacco Road*, and the serial *Terry and the Pirates*, before starring in his own series of films as Sergeant 'Dodo' Doubleday from 1941 to 1951.

In the 1950s and '60s, he turned his acting to the small screen, appearing on such shows as *Dragnet*, *The Westerner*, *The Life and Legend of Wyatt Earp* and *Perry Mason*.

William Tracy passed away, at the age of 50, on June 18, 1967, in Hollywood, California.

Publicity shot of William Tracy from
Angels with Dirty Faces (1938)

Lost Players

In my years of research on the kids, I have come across a few road blocks, such as dates of birth and death dates. The biggest question, however, is what happened to so and so after their movie career was over and what they did afterwards. I don't have the answer to some of these questions. These are the lost players; they have disappeared.

Eddie Brian

Eddie's first film role was in the Jackie Cooper film *Boy of the Streets* in 1938.

The one-time original East Side Kid also had roles in such films as *Boys Town*, *Angels with Dirty* Faces and *Scouts to the Rescue*. His last role on screen came in 1944 in the film *Youth Aflame*. Brian resurfaced for a short time in the 1950s, appearing on the small screen on such shows as *God's Children*, *Campbell Playhouse* and *West Point*.

Original East Side Kid, Eddie Brian

Jimmy Strand

Appearing in six East Side Kids films was about all Jimmy Strand did in his career. He made his first appearance in the series as a Cherry Street gang member. In 1944, he had two small uncredited roles, one being in the Jane Withers film *Faces in the Fog* and, his last, *Are These Our Parents?*, with Lyle Talbot. Then he vanished.

Jimmy Strand

Eddie Mills

Clancy Street Boys was the only East Side Kid film Eddie Mills would appear in. He would make only two more films as an actor before his career came to an end, *The Unknown Guest* (1943) with Victor Joy and *Her Highness and the Bellboy* with Hedy Lamarr (1945).

Authors' Note:

On July 30th 1945 during World War 2 the battle cruiser *USS Indianapolis*, which had just delivered components for the atomic bomb that would be dropped on Hiroshima, was torpedoed by a Japanese submarine; only 316 out of 1,200 men survived-Eddie Mills was not one of them.

Eddie Mills

William Frambes

Frambes, who played Homer in the first Bowery Boy film *Live Wires* (1946), made his first appearance in the East Side Kid film *Clancy Street Boys* as a Cherry Street gang member. From 1943 until 1952 he was in a total of thirty-two films, his last one being *The Pride of St. Louis*. His best role as an actor came in the *Janie* film series as Pvt. "Dead Pan" Hackett.

Left-William Frambes as Homer in *Live Wires*

Bill Channey

Save for playing the part of Tobey in the East Side Kid film *Block Busters*, very little is known of Bill Channey. He had a few minor roles in films, such as *Pride of the* Yankees and *Cinderella Jones* (Butch), and his last screen credits were for the small screen, including playing the part of Tex on the TV Western series *Wild Bill Hickok* (1956). Bill seems to have disappeared after this.

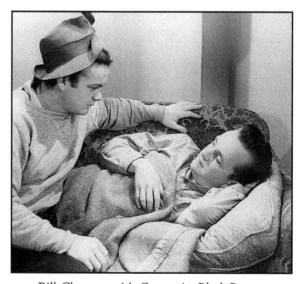

Bill Channey with Gorcey in *Block Busters*

Bill Bates

Bates' only tie to the East Side Kids is that he was in one of their films, *Ghosts on the Loose*, as Sleepy Dave, the organist. Other than that, he played a very minor role in Hitchcock's *Shadow of a Doubt* in 1943.

Bill Bates as Sleepy Dave

Leo Borden

With only four lines of dialogue in the film *Docks of New York*, Borden became an East Side Kid. His only other film roles were in *Twice Blessed* and *Joan of Arc*; both of these roles were uncredited.

Leo Borden in *Docks of New York*

Al Stone

Al Stone will be remembered as the obnoxious, pain-in-the-ass Herbie, Glimpy's cousin, in *Million Dollar Kid*. In 1949 he appeared on three episodes of Ed Sullivan's *Toast of the Town*.

Al Stone in *Million Dollar Kid*

Jimmy Murphy

Born Los Angeles, California, in 1935, Jim had dreams of being a world champion boxer. With a record of 19 wins and one loss, he seemed on his way, but while in the gym one day he was spotted by an agent who asked him if he was interested in acting. Knowing that acting paid more, he said yes.

Jimmy Murphy, as he appeared in the film *The Delicate Delinquent* (1957)

His first part was on the Annie Oakley TV show, and other roles quickly followed. He had parts in such films as *Blackboard Jungle* and *Cell 2455 Death Row*. Three of his best roles came in *Somebody Up There Likes Me*, *Mister Roberts* and *The Delicate Delinquent* with Jerry Lewis.

While trying to make ends meet as a struggling actor, he took a part-time job as a parking lot attendant, where a chance meeting with Leo Gorcey would lead to him being a Bowery Boy. Leo liked his face and thought that he would be a good fit in the series. Jim went on to appear in five Bowery Boy films as Myron.

During the '60s, '70s and '80s, Jim appeared on many TV show, such as *Peter Gunn*, *Quincy M.E.* and *Knight Rider*. It was also at this time that he became the road manager for Sammy Davis, Jr.

After completing a role on *Knight Rider* in 1985, he retired from acting. He has not resurfaced.

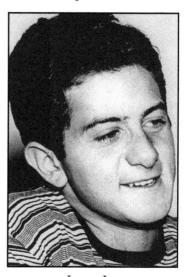

Lester Jay

Lester Jay

Lester Jay was in only one film *Little Tough Guys in Society* in 1938; his scenes in this film were cut, ending his hopes as a screen actor.

Lester's only claim to fame came when he played the part of Angel in the Road Company of the play Dead End, from 1936 until October 11th 1938, with stops in Washington and Chicago.

While in Chicago he found time to appear on radio, doing such shows like Lights Out, Rich Kid and the Rudy Vallee show.

This same year, 1938 Jay appeared on the show G I Jive (program-414) with the Joe Turner Blues Orchestra.

Jay passed away in 1997, in California.

Scene from *Little Tough Guys in Society* (1938) (left to right) Mischa Auer, Lester Jay, Harris Berger, Charles Duncan, Frankie Thomas, Hally Chester, Jackie Searl, David Gorcey sitting on the bed. Jay's scenes were later cut.

Photo Gallery

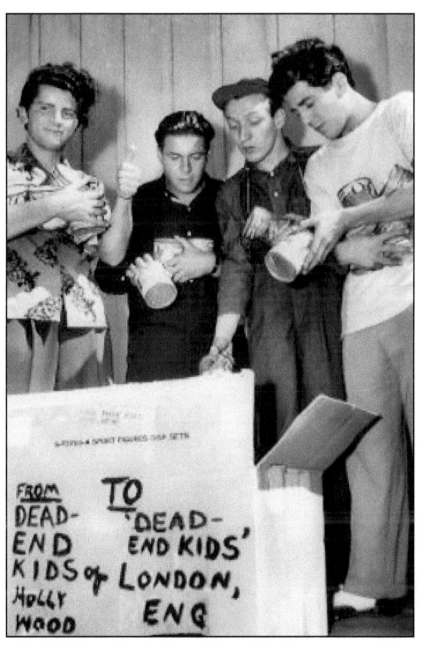

Gabe Dell, Bernard Punsly, Huntz Hall and Billy Halop prepare to load a case of goodies for youngsters in England, 1941.

Billy Halop, Gabe Dell, Bernard Punsly and Huntz Hall load cases of canned fish, chicken, ham and plum pudding bound for kids in London, 1941.

Ann Sheridan and Huntz Hall relax before shooting a scene for *The Angels Wash Their Faces*, 1939.

Above: Bernard Punsly (Top) and Hally Chester display tough kid poses in this publicity still from *Little Tough Guy*, 1938.

Left: Publicity pose of Billy Benedict in the role of Trouble in *Little Tough Guys in Society*, 1938.

On the Warner Brothers back lot during the making of *Crime School*, Gabe Dell and Leo Gorcey square off in a boxing match while Humphrey Bogart plays ref, 1938.

Above: Bernard Punsly finds time away from the set of *Crime School* on the Warner lot to do some practice shooting, 1938.

Left: "Tough Boy-Smart Boy, able to fight hard, talk fast and look tough, young David Gorcey believes these three qualities have helped establish him in boy hoodlum roles on screen." Publicity still from *Little Tough Guys in Society*, 1938.

Left: A little nonsense now and then is given by the toughest of the Dead End Kids— L. to R. Huntz Hall and wife Elsie May Anderson choke Billy Halop; Gabe Dell contributes to the festivities by strangling sister Ethel. The girls paid a visit to the gang during the filming of *Hit the Road*, 1941

Below: Cap-Bogart and the kids do their best Ring a Ding Ding on the Warners back lot, 1938

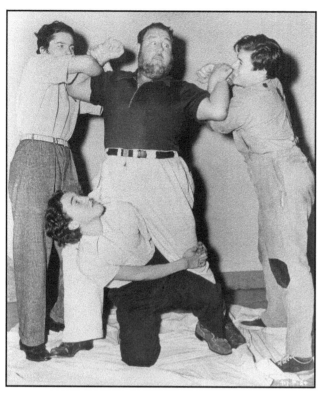

Man Mountain Dean looks as though he has met his match with (L. to R) Gabe Dell, Bernard Punsly and bottom Hally Chester, when he visited the set of *Little Tough Guy*, 1938.

Publicity still of Gabe Dell and Huntz Hall from *Hit the Road*, 1941.

"Roughing" the ball carrier is carried to a new extreme –Little Tough Guys Lester Jay, Hally Chester and (bottom) David Gorcey give Slapsie Maxie Rosenbloom the works during some practice play on the Universal studio back lot, 1938.

Huntz Hall and Bobby Jordan drink a milkshake while talking to Humphrey Bogart on the set of the film *Crime School*, 1938.

Above: (L to R) Bobby Jordan, Billy Halop, Leo Gorcey, Huntz Hall and Gabe Dell pose for a photo on the set of *Crime School*, 1938.

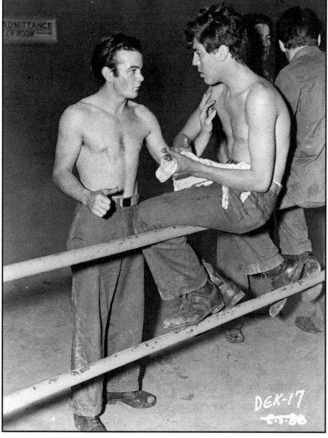

Left: Leo Gorcey seems to be telling Billy Halop he's the boss. (Foreground) Gabe Dell and Huntz Hall, 1938.

The Dead End Kids. Bobby Jordan, Gabe Dell, Humphrey Bogart, Huntz Hall, Bernard Punsly and Billy Halop give Leo Gorcey a lift up, 1938.

Publicity still of Peggy Stewart from *Little Tough Guy*, surrounded by tough kids with a heart of gold, Bernard Punsly, Hally Chester, Gabe Dell and Huntz Hall, 1938.

Huntz Hall, Gabe Dell, Bobby Jordan and Bernard Punsly do a little dance before singing
"Take Me Out to the Ballgame," 1938.

Huntz Hall, Gabe Dell, Bobby Jordan and Bernard Punsly being led off baseball field after singing their
version of "Take Me Out to the Ballgame," 1938.

Bobby Jordan, Bernard Punsly, Gabe Dell and Huntz Hall from 1938.

Billy Halop, Bobby Jordan, Gabe Dell, Huntz Hall and Bernard Punsly find different ways to have fun: roller skating on the Warner Brothers back lot, when on a lunch break from filming *The Angels Wash Their Faces*, 1939.

Pic -23-Cap- Huntz Hall, Billy Halop, Gabe Dell, Bernard Punsly and Bobby Jordan give their best pose of life in the 1900s, 1938.

Publicity shot of (top) Gabe Dell, Huntz Hall, Billy Halop, (bottom) Bernard Punsly, Bobby Jordan in their Sunday best for a scene in *Angels with Dirty Faces*, 1938.

Front row center, Johnny Downs, Ward Wood, Bobby Jordan and Billy Benedict entertain servicemen on the back lot of Universal Studios while filming the serial *Adventures of the Flying Cadets*, 1943.

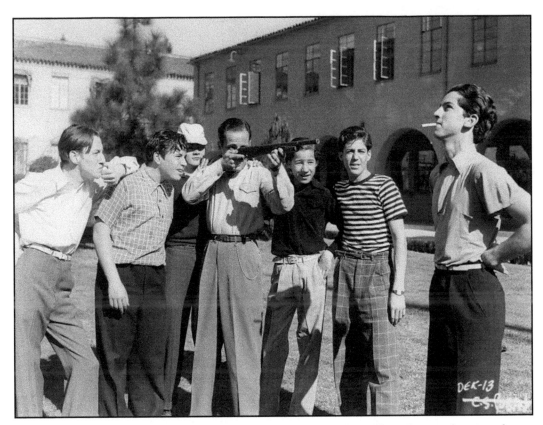

Humphrey Bogart takes dead aim at a cigarette or maybe Gabe Dell, with some free time from the set of *Crime School*, 1938.

Front cover of the July, 1941, issue of *Shadow Comics*, the Dead End Kids appeared in three issues of the comics, July-September-December, 1941. (Insert)

Graduating yearbook photo from Ken-Mar School in Hollywood, of Bernard Punsly, bottom left, from 1940.

From the Ken-Mar School in Hollywood, graduating class of 1940, top L. Harris Berger, bottom R. Ethel Dell

Above: Leo Gorcey and Bing Crosby in a scene from
Road to Zanzibar, 1941.

Left: Six faces of the
Dead End Kids, 1938.

The Feature Films

Dead End (Samuel Goldwyn / UA, August 27, 1937)

Variety (July 29, 1937):

Samuel Goldwyn has made a near-literal film translation of Sidney Kingsley's play, *Dead End*, New York stage success of the past two seasons…*Dead End* is a perfect technical job of reproducing the action of the play, with a few minor changes in the dialog from which some of the rough stuff has been deleted. What Goldwyn hasn't done is to enhance the message of the play by letting loose the full power of the screen as a form of art expression different from the drama. The Kingsley theme is that tenements breed gangsters, and no one does anything about it. The vicious cycle continues with each succeeding crop of children, thwarted in their growth of any sense of social responsibility by the pressure of vicious environment. The play whammed the idea across the footlights: the picture says and does everything the play said and did. And stops right there. There is no inventiveness or imaginative use of the cinema to develop the theme further, or wham it as hard as the play…Performances are uniformly fine, topped, of course, by the acting of the boy players from the New York production who seem better in the film because they do not crowd their lines so fast. Billy Halop, Huntz Hall, Bobby Jordan, Leo B. Gorcey, Gabriel Dell and Bernard Punsly all give splendid accounts of themselves.

Lobby card of the film *Dead End*

An artist drawing of the play *Dead End*.

Poster of Film *Dead End*

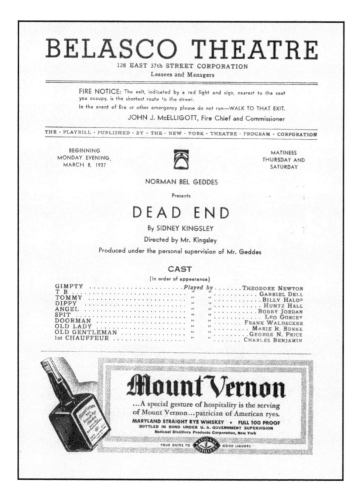

Inside cover of Playbill from the play *Dead End* (1937),
showing cast members

Halop, under ladder

Interior shot of Belasco Theatre

Kids arrive in Hollywood

Filming a scene, director William Wyler

Crime School (WB, May 28, 1938)

Variety (May 3, 1938)

When Sidney Kingsley finished with the Dead End boys, only one of them was on his way to the state reformatory. The others stood on the waterfront waiting for the day when the gang leader would come out and tell them all about it. They won't have to wait that long. Crane Wilbur puts the whole crew in reform school in his original screenplay, *Crime School*, which is a tense melodramatic film with a message of modern penology. It is rough entertainment, sometimes brutal, mostly interesting and exciting and should do good business where audiences like 'em tough…Some individual performances stand out like a welt on a 15-year-old back. Billy Halop and Leo Gorcey are the toughest mugs in the bunch. They and the other 'Dead Enders,' including Huntz Hall, Bernard Punsly and Gabriel Dell, give realistic impersonations. Bogart, who was a killer in the Goldwyn film version of *Dead End* is on the side of law and decency in *Crime School* and turns in a convincing job…*Crime School* is a virile, hard-hitting film.

Notes: One of the largest settings in the film was that of the lunch-dinner scence's where some 200 boys playing inmates of the reformatory were used as extras to fill the cafeteria, this scene took 3 days to shoot. For sequences showing the boys dining in the reformatory mess hall, 150 gallons of Irish stew, 750 loaves of braad, 100 gallons of coffie, two tons of potatoes, were provided. The 2nd largest set was that of the court yard in which the boys report for roll call, some 350-400 boy extras were used as Reform School Kids. The third largest set was a three-story reformatory in the form of an open square depickting the exercise yard. Complete with dormitories, dining halls, administration offices, reception rooms, covering one and one-half acres. The largest set built was the set representing the tenement district of New York's East Side…stores, flats and streets were struckted, covering two acres. To stock the stores and streets with items, 90 tons of mixed vegetables, canned goods, six crates of live chickens, 55 dressed turkeys, 400 sets of second-hand men's suits, five racks of women's dresses… 250 extras were used for street scenes. 50 gallons of pie filling/ paint were used to make Bernard

Cover of magazine, *Boy's Cinema*

Bogart and the kids on the back lot at Warner

Punsly a "lLiving Statue", along with 150 gallons of white wash paint were used to paint the dorm rooms.

The Dead End Kids wore out six sets of clothing during production, which began on January 29th, 1938 and concluded March 5.

After the release of this film, the contracts for Billy Halop, Huntz Hall, Gabriel Dell and Bernard Punsly were dropped (the contracts of Bobby Jordan and Leo Gorcey were retained). They were now able to freelance; they did, going over to Universal and making the film *Little Tough Guy*. Once the film *Crime School* was released and was a hit at the box office, all the boys' contracts

The Dead End Kids in a deleted scene

were renegotiated with a salary increase of $375 (from $275); they now were earning $650 per week. Mervyn LeRoy, who let the kids go, was fired by Warner Brothers and found employment at MGM.

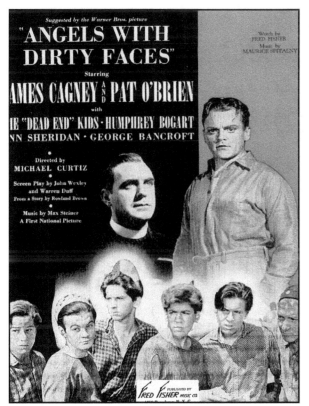

Angels with Dirty Faces (WB, November 24, 1938)

Variety (October 20, 1938):

Another typical Dead End Kids picture, but with the single exception that it has James Cagney and Pat O'Brien to bolster the dramatic interest and give box office draw…For Cagney the picture is likely to bring added prestige, for the bantam rooster of a racketeer is just the kind of part he plays best. He has a swagger and an aw-go-to-hell pugnacity that illumines a toughie characterization. That natural talent is accentuated in this yarn, particularly in his scrappy scenes with the 'Dead End Kids.' For once these young ruffians find their perfect match in screen arrogance, belligerence and plain orneriness. When Cagney slaps them around, he makes roughhouse stuff seem like superior pat-a-cake…Playing Cagney as a boy, Frankie Burke sounds so much like his grown-up self that the spectator might be pardoned for suspecting that the voice was dubbed.

Notes: Made at a cost of more than a million dollars, *Angels with Dirty Faces* was in production for eight weeks. The largest setting in the picture is the tenement street set. It covered four city blocks and was under construction for four weeks. Fifty-six pushcarts were brought in from New York to dress the set. While the street scenes were being made, a Burbank vegetable concern sold its entire stock to the studio each day. The vegetables, each evening, were distributed to charities.

Kids in pool room (autographed by David Durand). "All gamblers die brook."

Two thousand and forty different articles of clothing were used to dress the clotheslines on the roofs and fire escapes of the tenements. Two thousand rounds of machine-gun and revolver ammunition were fired in the gun battle scene.

During the filming of the scenes in the gas-filled warehouse, everyone in the company but O'Brien and Cagney wore gas masks. In one scene, Cagney stood at a window and real machine-gun bullets were fired over his head into a wall.

It took three days to "electrocute" Cagney. So emotional was the scene that he lost four pounds. The studio copied the famous chair at Sing, Sing prison for the picture, but it was never photographed. Only its shadow was shown against a wall.

The longest take in the film took place in the death

(with hat) Marilyn Knowlden, Frankie Burke and William Tracy.

cell between Cagney and O'Brien and lasted for twelve minutes. The two stars made the long scene, without one mistake, the first time.

Director Curtiz nicknamed the six Dead End kids "the mad Russians." He had detectives watching them throughout the picture to see that they were in bed early. He put up a fifty-dollar prize to the boy who behaved himself best and Billy Halop won the prize. The kids gave Curtiz a scroll signed in blood the final day of shooting.

It was O'Brien's father who discovered young actor William Tracy to portray his son in the film when he saw his work in the film *Brother Rat*.

Frankie Burke, who plays the young Cagney, impersonated Cagney for four years in the hope of getting into pictures. He had finally given up the idea and was a bellhop in a hotel in Vegas when he learned of the search for a youth and got the job.

They Made Me a Criminal (WB, January 28, 1939)

Variety (January 20, 1939):

The picture is a carefully prepared and skillfully produced effort that should rate as absorbing if undistinguished entertainment for general appeal. Story is familiar enough—a reworking of several standard plot formulas. Concerns a newly-crowned middleweight champ who sobers up from his victory celebration to discover he's supposed to have been killed in an auto crash after murdering a newspaper reporter. He slinks away to Arizona, where he makes his home on a fruit ranch, becomes the hero of the Dead End Kids, who have been sent from New York's slums to be regenerated, and falls in love with the sister of one of the boys…Of the supporting players, the Dead End Kids repeat their rowdy stuff in a new setting, fitting into the story nicely and proving an effective foil for [John] Garfield.

Notes: The film was a remake of *The Life of Jimmy Dolan*, which was based on the play *Sucker*. *They Made Me a Criminal* was in production for ten weeks and was literally filmed on the run. Six different locations were used, and more than 40 different sets were constructed on the Warner Brothers back lot. Director Busby Berkeley first took his troupe to Garnet, California, for scenes to be shot of moving railroad cars. Then it was off to the North Los Angeles Railroad Station for more scenes. The third location Berkeley traveled to was the Jim

Lobby card

Crew wears protective gear netting while filming scene.

Kids help Garfield take a shower.

Jeffries Barn, a fight arena near Burbank, California. Also used for fight scenes was the new Hollywood American Legion Stadium at the studio. The fifth location used was the huge irrigation tank of an orange grove near Whittier, California; the tank was used as a swimming pool for the near-drowning (Bobby Jordan) sequence. Next, the company moved to a large date garden near Indio, California, 14 miles from Palm Springs; this location was used for two weeks. For the sixth and final location, it was back to the rail yards, where Garfield's most dangerous scenes were shot. Garfield had to run along the top of a rapidly moving freight train, jumping from car to car.

Chief of Berkeley's concerns while filming in the desert was to make it comfortable for 70-year-old May Robson. The temperatures at midday reached 130-degrees, and never dropping below 80 at night. The staff started filming each morning at 5:00 a.m. and quit shortly after noon each day. The days of filming in the sunlight made it perfect for cameraman James Wong Howe, the master of photographic light and shadows.

Bobby Jordan was the first of three to be heat stricken within 15 minutes of one another; he collapsed as he played a scene. Dr. Don Hill's fever thermometer registered 107-degrees, but Jordan reported for work the next morning.

Besides the heat being a problem, the cast and crew had to deal with crickets and millions of gnats; the cricket problems were solved with a foot. As for the gnat situation, property man George Sweeney solved it by purchasing several yards of black mosquito netting, which was worn by cast and crew over the head and down over the face and tied securely around the neck. This at least protected them from the flying insects. The cast only removed them when shooting a scene.

Bobby Jordan boxing with Huntz Hall.

Extras, totaling more than 1,000 in number, were used at various times for spectators in fight scenes, sidewalk pedestrians and town folk. Ten times that number of box lunches was consumed because of the many location calls.

During the three days that it took to film the wild party scenes, Garfield, Ann Sheridan, Barbara Pepper and Robert Glecker drank three cases of ginger ale.

The crew for this film was 100 and started filming under conditions far from ideal from a standpoint of personal comfort; perfect, however, for beauty and uniqueness of setting.

Hell's Kitchen (WB, July 8, 1939)

Variety (July 1, 1939):
Hell's Kitchen is another meller with the Dead-End lads. Chief difference here is that it shows the bunch in a 'shelter for boys,' a la Boys Town...The 'Dead–End Kids' chip in with several moving performances but are permitted to mug too frequently.

Notes: Twenty-five locations, including the Pan-Pacific ice-skating rink, were used and thirty-eight sets at the studio. The most important location was the McKinley Home for Boys, in the San Fernando Valley. Two hundred and thirty boys from the home were used as extras for filming.

Hockey scenes were filmed at the Pan-Pacific skating rink, where some 200 extras were used, along with the U.S.C. varsity hockey team, who also gave the Dead End Kids instructions on how to skate.

Halop and Jordan

Publicity still of Punsly, Halop, Grant Mitchell, Dell, Gorcey and Hall.

Publicity still of Jordan with
Tippie the dog.

Fifty loafs of bread, 35 gallons of milk, 20 boxes of vegetables and 10 gallons of potatoes were consumed on a daily basis.

The clever dog in the picture, Tippie, age five months, was the youngest trained canine in Hollywood, out of 260 dog actors.

The Angels Wash Their Faces (WB, August 26, 1939) (Working Title: *Battle of City Hall*)

Variety (September 2, 1939):

Newest 'Dead End' melodramatic adventure sacrifices plausibility for action, but Ray Enright's terrific meller pace makes it the sort of fare the average audience will eat up. Surefire box office in spots where they like Ann Sheridan and the 'Dead End' Kids, and doubtlessly will do sturdy biz in other houses…Besides the familiar characterizations by the Dead-End group of six, Frankie Thomas and Bonita Granville figure importantly.

Notes: At the beginning of production, Ann Sheridan was declared the "Oomph Girl" by a committee of thirty men of the world, including the Earl of Warwick, Dick Powell, Robert L. Ripley, Eddie Cantor, Ray Noble, Fred MacMurray and Earl Carroll. The new "Oomph Girl" was subjected to some innocent 'gags' over her new honor by the six Dead End Kids.

Poster of film

Publicity still of Punsly, Hall and Jordan making moves on Ann Sheridan.

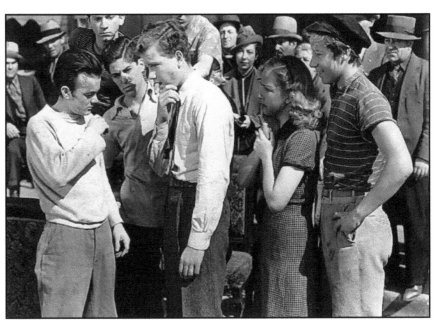

Gorcey, Halop, Frankie Thomas, Bonita Granville, Jordan.

Stunts included raising her car on a platform and placing a sign on it that read, "The Oomph Girl must sell this car at once to meet a note."

The toughness of the kids was somewhat lacking in this picture; they were now members of a "club" instead of a "gang" and they all were dressed in their best during sequences showing them as city officials.

The Burbank, California, fire department was used in the fire scenes, filmed over a three-night period.

Frankie Thomas launched his new 36-foot auxiliary sloop, *Mona*, named after his mother, at the Wilmington harbor. Jackie Searl competed in many steeplechase exhibitions and won a blue ribbon when not on the set.

On Dress Parade (WB, November 18, 1939)

Variety (October 27, 1939):
While their last flicker, 'Angels Wash Their Faces,' removed something of the Dead End Kids' bad-boy onus, current release apparently marks their finis as the appealing gang from the far side of the tracks. They're cleaned up, brushed up, put in military school uniforms, turned into refined little gentlemen - and it's too bad. It's too bad, at least that if the transition had to be made it should be in such a mawkishly sentimental and obvious picture. It just doesn't ring true. To the credit of the gang, they make of an impossible story a passable picture for dualers. To retain the kids' b.o.

Poster for film

Jordan and Hall

value, however, Warner Brothers will certainly have to do better than this for them in the future. They are talented, individually and collectively, and if satisfactory story material can't be devised for them as a group, it might be wise to forget them as an entity and use one or two of them at a time. It's obvious that they can't go on forever as little toughies - especially in as-much as they're getting to be rather grown-up toughies now - so perhaps the quicker the breakup and weeding out begins the better. Of the six Dead-enders four are totally reformed in the current yarn and Leo 'Spit' Gorcey succumbs before the final bell. Bernard Punsly, in a bit, is the only one who manages to retain his dese-dem-and-dose.

Notes: The working title for this film was *The Dead End Kids at Valley Forge* due to the fact that technical advisor John Murphy was a graduate of Valley Forge Military Academy.

Hall, Dell, and Jordan

The vast number of sets representing interiors and exteriors of the fictitious military school were constructed just for this film. These included classrooms, dormitory rooms, a huge mess hall (capable of feeding several hundred boys) and sections of the huge academy campus.

The sham battle sequences were filmed on the 4,200-acre Warner Brothers ranch in Calabasas, California. More than 5,000 rounds of live ammunition were fired during the sham battle.

Marching and dress parade sequences were filmed on the grounds of the Los Angeles Cricket Club in Griffith Park. The Dead End Kids claimed to have walked more than 100 miles in less than a week learning how to drill like cadets.

A complete military camp was laid out at the ranch for summer camp scenes. The kids sang the old song "You're in the Army Now," but in swing style. Director [William] Clemens liked what he heard, and used their version.

When it came time for the kids to get their military haircuts, Frankie Thomas didn't object; he was glad to get rid of his thick, curly hair.

Principals and extras consumed more than 200 pounds of baked ham, 40 gallons of milk, sixteen gallons of mashed potatoes and about fifty crates of lettuce, tomatoes and a gross of hard rolls in the mess hall scenes. Prop men had difficulty in keeping the kids from eating between scenes. The food was prepared in a kitchen set up on a soundstage.

Punsly and Gorcey in an early scene

During the filming Bernard Punsly graduated from Fairfax High School with the highest grades possible to attain.

The kids won some money ($150) when studio workers thought that they had found a movie mistake in the script. On a statue of Nathan Hale used in the film, it read "My only regret is that I have but one life to lose for my country." Workers thought it should be "give" and not "lose," but research proved the kids right.

Little Tough Guy (Universal, July 22, 1938)

Variety (August 17, 1938):
This one is merely a rehash of 'Dead End' and 'Crime School' again featuring the young toughies known as the 'Dead End Kids.' It's a weakie for single-billing and its 83 minutes running time is of embarrassing length for the duals. Word-of-mouth will be negligible…Of course the unredeemable flaw in 'Little Tough Guy' is that it's merely a rubber stamp of

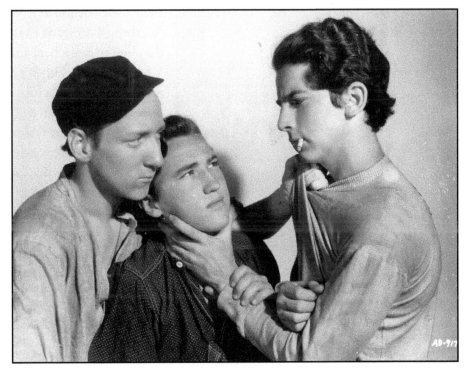

Hall, Chester, Dell

Hall, Halop and Helen Parrish

Halop and Gorcey

'Crime School,' which was in turn more or less of a rubber stamp of 'Dead End.' At least all three have the same brawling principals and identical atmosphere and mood…As the principals of the opus, the kids are themselves—which is to say they're forthright, hard-hitting and effective.

Notes: Two hundred schoolboys were hired by Universal Studios to help the Dead End Kids in the riot fight scenes; the kids turned a settlement house into a complete wreck. In the heat of the fight scene, director Harold Young was punched in the mouth, resulting in the loss of a tooth. Property damage from the fight included twenty-seven broken chairs, six broken windows and one door torn from its hinges.

During this film the Dead End Kids came up with their own vocabulary. When Billy Halop calls a person "a creep," he means that the person is a bad character, a double-crosser, a heel and "a rat." The word "Lut" means a person is silly. Other phrases used by the kids: "Crum," a worthless fellow, a louse; "Sizzer," a pretty girl, a knock-out, a sizzling beauty; "Umphy," a smart person, a fast stepper, knows everything; "Mickeys," roast Irish potatoes, grub, simple food; "Gooch," a chiseler, sponger, a weak sister; "Noodler," anyone educated, a dandy, a college graduate; "Miffer," a wild goose chase, futile attempt, wasted effort.

Richard Selzer, better known as fashion designer Blackwell, who has the very minor role of Bud, has claimed for years that he was once a member of the Dead End Kids. Not True.

Call a Messenger (Universal, November 3, 1939)

Variety (November 9, 1939):

Billy Halop and Huntz Hall, leaders from the Dead End Kids group, are given a chance to shine in this new semi-gangster picture. Pair give more legitimate performances than customary, and cash in on this chance. Their work and the presence of several veterans go far in making familiar material and impossible situations click. Result is a rowdy, gripping production patterned for theatres such as this one and as heavy bolstering in dual set-ups…Billy Halop grabs off leading honors as the lad who makes something of himself and his sister. Huntz Hall is an excellent foil and races veteran El Brendel for comedy laurels.

Berger, Chester, Hall, Halop, Benedict, and Gorcey deliver a love message

Halop, Benedict, Gorcey, Hall, Berger and Chester

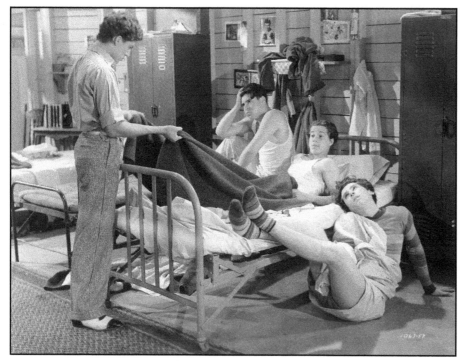

Halop, Punsly, Jordan, Dell.

You're Not So Tough (Universal, July, 26, 1940)

Variety (July 8, 1940):

Remnants of the Dead End Kids and the Little Tough Guys, making up a group of five young squirts, are a very tiresome and boring lot in Kem Goldsmith's production built around them and a couple of other characters in *You're Not So Tough*...Audiences could probably get along without any more of these brats and their stale antics...Unless the slapping and socking, throwing things and the like, by the tough kids can be construed as funny, the picture has very little comedy relief...An unintended laugh, however, is the way little Halop socks a couple of grownups who look big enough to take on Jack Dempsey. Dialog ordinary, much of it in the gutter groove.

Hall plays cowboys and Indians with Halop.

Junior G-Men (Universal, 12-Chapter Serial, August 1940)

Chapter (1) Enemies Within
Chapter (2) The Blast of Doom
Chapter (3) Human Dynamite
Chapter (4) Blazing Danger
Chapter (5) Trapped by Traitors
Chapter (6) Traitor's Treachery
Chapter (7) Flaming Death
Chapter (8) Hurled Through Space
Chapter (9) The Plunge of Peril
Chapter (10) The Toll of Treason
Chapter (11) Descending Doom
Chapter (12) The Power of Patriotism

Variety (August 9, 1940):

Basic plot has the Dead End Kids battling the forces of evil in this 12-chapter serial led by Billy Halop…They find that an anarchist band called the "Order of the Flaming Torch," led by Cy Kendall as Brand, is bent on destroying military projects. The boys play detectives and keep on the trail of the traitor suspects.

Give Us Wings (Universal, December 20, 1940)

Variety (November 7, 1940):

The ambitions of a group of tough kids to become air pilots provides sufficient story foundation to carry this moderate budgeter through the secondary duals as supporting feature, especially with the action and juvenile trade…Tied in with present air training of youth, the picture is of current interest. Story follows obvious dramatic lines, with plenty of slapstick horseplay among the boys injected to keep the picture from going static…Direction by Charles Lamont over-emphasizes both the dramatic and comedy passages, with all of the boys doing plenty of mugging and double-takes.

Halop, Hall and Anne Gwynne

Jordan, Hall, Milburn Stone, Punsly, Dell, Wallace Ford, and Shemp Howard

Hit the Road (Universal, June 27, 1941)

Variety (July 2, 1941):

Answer to that frequently-put query, "What's wrong with the picture industry?" might well be that the Dead End Kids are out of the reformatory again. They seem perpetually to have just been released from cells, and each time some hard-pressed studio ups and celebrates the event by making a picture about them…Formula is always the same, and 'Hit the Road' is no exception. It's a less-than-mild supporter for the duals…This time, as has been done before, remnants of the Dead Enders have been parlayed with a couple of brats from a rival group, The Little Tough Guys. The combination, aside from 10-year-old Bobs Watson, provides as unpalatable a cast as a film can have. Add to that the confused and preposterous story and the lack of b.o. appeal becomes obvious.

The kids play with dynamite. Halop, Dell, Punsly, and Hall.

Publicity still with Dell, Halop, and Hall.

Sea Raiders (Universal, 12-Chapter Serial, August 1941)

Chapter (1) The Raider Strikes
Chapter (2) Flaming Torture
Chapter (3) The Tragic crash
Chapter (4) The Raider Strikes Again
Chapter (5) Flames of Fury
Chapter (6) Blasted from the Air
Chapter (7) Victims of the Storm
Chapter (8) Dragged to Their Doom
Chapter (9) Battling the Beast
Chapter (10) Periled by a Panther
Chapter (11) Entombed in a tunnel
Chapter (12) Paying the Penalty

Variety (August 3, 1941):
    This Dead End Kid entry has the kids seeking the identity of the "Sea Raider" who has been sinking Allied ships.

Mob Town (Universal, October 3, 1941)

Variety (September 30, 1941):
    Another in a series Universal is turning out with some of the Dead End Kids, 'Mob Town' is synthetically-contrived and overly-theatric tale of East Side toughies on the loose…Burdened with script of grammar school caliber, picture is a filler for secondary duals…Attempt to mix up dramatics and comedy does a curdle, with inadequate scripting obvious throughout…The tough kids mug and overact to accentuate the synthetic dialog provided.

Scene with Punsly, Hall, Halop, Dick Foran, John Butler.

The Kids fight it out in this one: Halop, Punsly, Hall and

Junior G-Men of the Air (Universal, 12-Chapter Serial, June 1942)

Chapter (1) Wings Aflame
Chapter (2) The Plunge of Peril
Chapter (3) Hidden Danger
Chapter (4) The Tunnel of Terror
Chapter (5) The Black Dragon Strikes
Chapter (6) Flaming Havoc
Chapter (7) The Death Mist
Chapter (8) Satan Fires the Fuse
Chapter (9) Satanic Sabotage
Chapter (10) Trapped in a Blazing 'Chute'
Chapter (11) Undeclared War
Chapter (12) Civilian Courage Conquers

Variety (May 20, 1942):

Juve thriller for Saturday matinee billing is the standard scalp-lifting stuff with a gesture toward current themes…It's transparently ludicrous to adults, but is sufficiently packed with explosive action, villainy and heroics to keep the urchins in a dither. It even has what the kids will regard as comedy…Basic plot has the Dead End Kids and Little Tough Guys, headed by Billy Halop, as non-conformist rapscallions obsessed with being flyers. They become involved in the machinations of an espionage-sabotage ring and the State Patrol and the Junior G-Men…There are slugfests, wild chases, dizzy plane flights and such roughhouse galore. The story is strictly ersatz (the scenarists aren't even billed, probably at their own request), while the direction, acting, photography and special effects are really dire. But youngsters will surely gulp every frenzied moment of it.

Tough As They Come (Universal, June 5, 1942)

Variety (June 3, 1942):

Ex-juvenile Ape (Bernard Punsly) is training for a boxing career with friends Pig (Huntz Hall) and String (Gabriel Dell). Their old gang leader Tommy Clark (Billy Halop), now a law student, is offered a job with the crooked Apex Finance Company, from his girlfriend's father. The Dead End Kids are growing up in this one and not a minute too soon.

Punsly takes up boxing with John Gallaudet and Dell

Dell, Halop, Hall, and Punsly

Mug Town (Universal, January 22, 1943)

Variety (January 14, 1943):

This is another in the Universal group of dramas built around remnants of the Dead End Kids. Without too much stress on either originality or credulity, picture still retains sufficient dramatics of type

Poster for *Mug Town*

to pass as supporting dualer in the secondary houses where previous issues have been accepted. Story is forced in attempting to display further antics of the recalcitrant tough guys…Halop, Huntz Hall, Bernard Punsly and Gabriel Dell comprise the youthful knights of the road, performing in regular style with usual overlay of mugging. Attempts to inject comedy through silly routines handed Hall are decidedly sophomoric.

Notes: This was Billy Halop's and Bernard Punsly's last film as Dead End Kids; they both enlisted in the Army after shooting their final scenes. Also of note, none of the Little Tough Guys were present in this film.

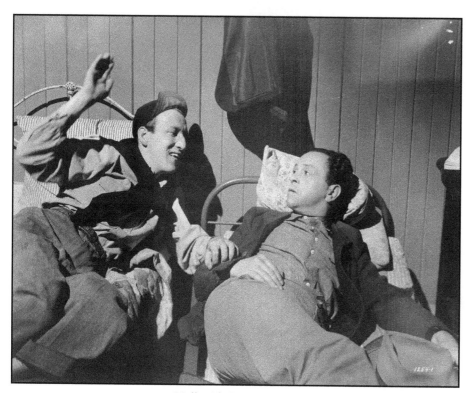

Hall with Danny Beck

Keep 'Em Slugging (Universal, August 2, 1943)

Variety (February 25, 1943):

Again parading the antics and dramatics of Universal's Dead End Kids and Little Tough Guys, 'Keep 'Em Slugging' follows familiar formula for previous issues in the series. Cranked out on low budget, it's a supporter for duals that have found customers receptive to this type of product. There's little originality in either the story, comedic horseplay of the tough youths or the dramatics unreeled. To get in wartime step, the four boys—Huntz Hall, Bobby Jordan, Gabriel Dell and Norman Abbott—seek jobs for summer vacations.

Notes: The Little Tough Guys were absent from this last entry in the Dead End Kids film series. This is the only time in Bobby Jordan's film career that he was the leader of the Dead End Kids. Replacing Bernard Punsly in this film was Norman Abbott, the nephew of Bud Abbott; it was his only film as a Dead End Kid.

Jordan, Norman Abbott, Dell and Shemp Howard.

Milburn Stone, Jordan, and Elyse Knox

Little Tough Guys in Society (Universal, November 20, 1938)

Variety (November 19, 1938):

A production of no more than passing importance, 'Little Tough Guys in Society' will disappoint if pushed into dates where better than average programmers are demanded. The picture is not for larger first runs nor does it suit as the No. 1 feature in dualers of top grade. Down the line in lesser single billers and for secondary duals, it should prove suitable...This time Universal's six Little Tough Guys are placed in a different setting, that of a country estate which they virtually wreck before picking up a little religion. Story is implausible and the plot inconsistent, but here and there the dialog is sprightly. At other times it is tiresome, particularly the East Side chatter of the toughies. The boring, slow-going plot is offset somewhat by comedy situations, but not so much by the slapstick or stunts in which the kids figure. It's through Edward Everett Horton, Mischa Auer and Mary Boland...Some of the pranks of the six Little Tough Guys are a bit amusing, but much of the slapstick they indulge belongs to third-rate vaude or shorts. East side ruffians are Frankie Thomas, Hally Chester, Harris Berger, Charles Duncan, David Gorcey and William Benedict. They overplay a trifle, and some of the bullying by one of the lads, the leader, is carried too far to be believable. Most kids wouldn't take what he hands out, particularly if they're supposed to be tough. Popularity of the six Little Tough Guys (offshoot, in part, of the already overdone Dead End Kids) for film purposes probably will

The Little Tough Guys All dressed up. (From left): Berger, Chester, Gorcey, Benedict, Duncan, Thomas

The Little Tough Guys don't look like they are on their best behavior. (Left) Gorcey, Thomas, Duncan; (bottom) Chester, Berger, and Benedict.

be short-lived anyway, particularly if the material isn't better than in this instance. There's nothing likable about any of them or anything that's entertaining.

Notes: Lon "Buddy" McCallister was originally signed to play the part of Danny, the leader of the Little Tough Guys, in this film, but wasn't right for the tough-kid role and replaced by Frankie Thomas.

Newsboys' Home (Universal, January 22, 1939)

Variety (January 21, 1939):
Another in the tough kid cycle. The rehash is a newspaper theme, and Hollywood's usual far-fetched presentation of the fourth estate is gone one better with this entry, which pictures the circulation side as being little short of a World War, with the kids in the middle of it all. Implausible most of the way, youngsters will eat it up while envisioning themselves in same situations, etc. Will easily handle its end of dual depots, what with revitalized Jackie Cooper name, Edmund Lowe, and the word of mouth. Plot is very thin, and acting of all but the kids similarly light. Moral seems to be that yellow journalism pays and that woman has no place at the head of a newspaper. Entire reel rests heavily on the antics of the rowdy Little Tough Guys and ringleader Cooper.

Notes: Jackie Cooper worked with former East Side Kid David Durand in two films, *Streets of New York* (1939) and the serial *Scouts to the Rescue* (1939). Cooper, along with Elisha Cook, Jr., only worked with the kids in this film.

Publicity still with Elisha Cook Jr., Chester, Duncan, Benedict, and Gorcey

Gorcey, Benedict, Elisha Cook, Jr., Chester, Duncan, Jackie Cooper

Code of the Streets (Universal, April, 17, 1939)

Variety (April 15, 1939):

Although the story fabric is not new, 'Code of the Streets' gives a new slant on juvenile delinquents and what can be done with them on the screen. Picture looks like another moneymaker for Universal. The 'Little Tough Guys' live up to their previous record as box-office, good enough to stand on its own in certain houses where they go for hoke melodrama, and fine support on most double bill alignments. Has 'Tough Guys' band playing amateur Sherlocks. While again incorporating the usual appeal for juvenile trade, story blends the activities of east side hoodlums with a moving mobster fable...Director Harold Young displays nicety of balance between the more action-ful episodes, the braggadocio of the kid mob and the mystery element. He is helped materially by two slick performances from Frankie Thomas, as the ex-detective's son, and James McCallion, as head of the 'little toughies' and brother of the condemned man...Harris Berger, Hally Chester, Charles Duncan, William Benedict and David Gorcey, as the 'Little Tough Guys,' show up as well as the last time out after they get over their initial

Publicity still with Duncan, Chester, Berger, Frankie Thomas, Harry Carey, Gorcey, Benedict, and McCallion.

Scene with (top) Gorcey, Chester, McCallion, Thomas, (bottom) Berger, Duncan and Benedict

overacting…Be on the lookout for David Gorcey, and Charles Duncan should go far with better roles.

Notes: During my conversations with Jimmy McCallion, he told me that Universal was going to make a total of five Little Tough Guy features, but only three were made. If Universal would have made the five as planned, he was the going to be the leader of the kids in the last two.

Also in our conversations, he mentioned how the contract negotiations for the last two films between Charles Duncan (who thought he was a big star, according to Mr. McCallion), Hally Chester, Harris Berger, Billy Benedict, David Gorcey and himself fell through because of their request of a $175-per-week raise; they were making $350 at the time. Their request for more money was not met, so they all walked.

The East Side Kids (Four-Bell Production / Monogram, February, 10, 1940)

Starring the Original East Side Kids

Variety (February 15, 1940):

What suggests a road company of the Dead Enders is presently masquerading as the 'Original East Side Kids' in this Monogram film, another in the long series of sociological experiments in adolescent reformation. In telling of society's means to rehabilitate youngsters whose environs on the city streets don't permit them the proper atmosphere to bridge the gap between childhood and adulthood, Monogram has turned out an absurdly poor picture that will command little interest from even the vast army of Dead End-type devotees. Wherein the' original 'billing is concerned, the film has somewhat confusing selling angle in its theoretical association with the Dead End Kids. However, it won't make any difference in the long run. Where their prototypes are involved, the East Siders run a decidedly poor second, and one can bet

Scene from *East Side Kids*, with Leon Ames, Joyce Bryant, Berger, Burke, Alden Chase

a good stiffbelt in the slats that Leo Gorcey, Bobby Jordan, et al. would whale the stuffings out of the East Siders. It's all a strained atmosphere of kids schooled in the ways of crime and their ultimate reformation after a dull chase for counterfeiters, in which they join after first being accessories.

Boys of the City (Four-Bell Production / Monogram, July 15, 1940)

Variety (August 17, 1940):
    Two of the original Dead End Kids and a flock of extra toughies form the East Side Kids for this film, a weak runoff. Reels are crammed full with faults in photography, direction, story and emoting: yet when caught a full house seemed to enjoy Leo Gorcey, Bobby Jordan and company wrassling a mystery, the reason for which is never clearly explained, to a conclusion. For duals.

    Notes: As recent as 2006, in the book *From Broadway to the Bowery* by Len Getz, the review for cast credits is incorrect. Also incorrect is the cast credits from *Variety*'s 1940 review of this film. Both *Variety* and Getz have the parts for certain players inaccurately listed.

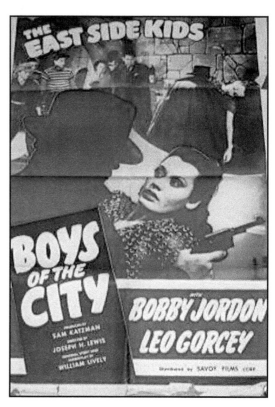

Getz's has the following mistakes:
    1. Algie, played by Jack Edwards—should be part played by Eugene Francis
    2. Ike, played by David Gorcey— no one in the cast goes by this name!
    3. Gorcey played the part of Peewee.
    4. PeeWee played by Frankie Burke—should be part played by David Gorcey.
    5. PeeWee played by Frankie Burke—he played the part of Peter.

Morrison, Gorcey, Haines, Chester, David Gorcey, Burke, Jordan watch
Eugene Francis and Dave O'Brien change a tire.

Some errors found in *Variety* are as follows:
1. Algie played by Jack Edwards —should be part played by Eugene Francis
2. Boy played by Hally Chester —should be Johnny played by Hally Chester.
3. Skinny played by Frankie Burke — should be part played Donald Haines.
4. PeeWee played by Donald Haines—should be part played by David Gorcey.
5. David Gorcey is omitted from *Variety's* review.

That Gang of Mine (Four-Bell Production / Monogram, September 23, 1940)

Variety (December 26, 1940):

Racetrack stories and the exploits of the Dead End Kids are both leavening off but aside from that, Sam Katzman's production of *That Gang of Mine* is so generally lacking in merit that it will have trouble getting dates, either in number or quality. The double-billers, which require a lot of product and buy virtually everything that comes along, looks like its best market. Katzman obviously has not spent a lot of money on this picture, with result it may come out on the right side of the ledger for producer and distributor regardless of its lack of entertainment value, production quality or story treatment…Action is dragged out to the point of boredom with detail, and the antics of the Dead Enders for apparent purposes of comedy value prove irksome quickly. The tough kids with their gutter manners and wisecracking are still far from being sympathetic characters…A veteran of the Dead Enders working closely with Gorcey is Bobby Jordan, whom Grandma wouldn't want around the house for long. Others in the group are Donald Haines, David Gorcey and Sunshine Sammy Morrison, a colored kid who could be used to better advantage.

Clarence Muse, Gorcey, director Joseph H. Lewis, Sam Katzman

Filming a scene for *That Gang of Mine*

Pride of the Bowery (Banner Production / Monogram, January 24, 1941)

Variety (January 24, 1941):

The uniforms are different but the plot's the same - and even a few of the faces are familiar. Last summer Columbia sent the Dead End Kids (a remnant of the originals) to military academy; now Monogram sends the East Side Kids (still a remnant of the Dead-Enders) to a CCC camp. And writers Steven Clensos and George Plympton have scarcely bothered to change an iota of the plot except for the locale. Result is a hackneyed story that telegraphs its way almost from the opening scene and will scarcely please those who remember 'Military Academy.' For the others, it will be acceptable enough for B support in minor situations. Tale is straightforwardly told with pleasing simplicity and with more than adequate thespic and directorial skill. Leo Gorcey, who appeared to have been completely reformed in military school, is reformed all over again at the Government's expense in the current vehicle. His lineup of supporters includes Bobby Jordan, one of the original tough film moppets, and a couple of newcomers who satisfactorily fit into the scheme of things.

Notes: Bobby Stone makes his first appearance in this film as Willie.

Haines, Gorcey, Jordan, David Gorcey arrive at CCC Camp

Publicity still for *Pride of the Bowery*

Flying Wild (Banner Production / Monogram, March 10, 1941)

Variety (April 11, 1941)

For some reason not readily apparent, the brash youngsters formerly called the Dead End Kids have been re-tabbed the East Side Kids for this Monogram production. All the same, 'Flying Wild' is just one more in the by-now-at-tenuated lineup of Dead End Kids action pictures. Its class C stuff for the marquee, or as a prospect for critical reaction, word-of-mouth or box-office pull. This time five young rapscallions, two of whom are apparently from the original Dead End mob, tangle with and ultimately hog-tie a gang of saboteurs trying to block production at and steal blueprints from an aircraft factory. When the picture isn't banging out-of-the-corner-of-the-mouth wisecracks at the audience, it's straining the credulity with laboriously contrived story construction. Leo Gorcey and Bobby Jordan are featured as ex-Dead End ringleaders. They give such accurately-remembered performances that the dialog gives the impression of having been lifted from some of their past pictures.

Notes: Eugene Francis left the series after the completion of this film for military service.

David Gorcey, Morrison, unidentified actor, Leo Gorcey, Jordan, Francis, Haines, and Stone

Bowery Blitzkrieg (Banner Production / Monogram, September 8, 1941)

Variety (September 30, 1941):
Parts of the old Dead End Kids troupe, now known as East Side Kids, have grown up. And so has their story material. Both represent an improvement, plainly evident in 'Bowery Blitzkrieg,' which is lots better than the title indicates. Film best geared for dual consumption and will be a pleaser. The Bowery rowdies don't veer far from the familiar pattern in this one, excepting for emphasis on the amateur fight game. Per usual, the yarn shows one of the Dead Enders ditching the straight-and-narrow for quick profits though petty stickups. The toughie, Leo Gorcey, is reformed by developing his fistic prowess in the Golden Gloves amateur fights...Gorcey, as Muggs, Bowery rowdy who straightens out his hectic life by becoming an amateur champ, does a good job. Huntz Hall, as his manager, is elevated into more prominence, measuring up nicely in his heavier assignment. Bobby Jordan is the other Bowery boxer who is saved from going completely bad by a policeman's effort and the loyalty of his former

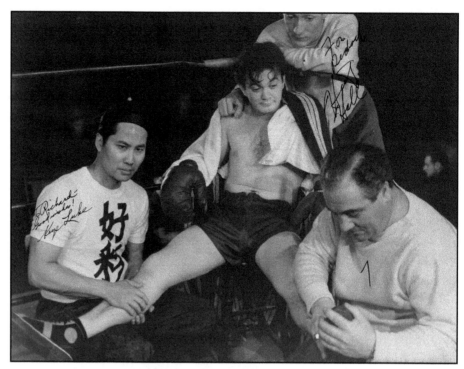

Scene from *Bowery Blitzkrieg* with Keye Luke, Gorcey, Hall and Pat Costello

Haines, Gorcey, Hall, and Stone

pals...Bobby Stone, David Gorcey and Ernest Morrison are good in supporting roles.

Notes: A new member to the East Side Kids, Huntz Hall played the part of Glimpy in the next sixteen films.

Spooks Run Wild (Banner Production / Monogram, October 24, 1941)

Variety (November 1, 1941):

Okay supporting fodder for nabes and other subsequent situations, this hokey, though evenly balanced, mixture of chills and comedy should prove a winner with the juvenile trade in particular. All the familiar tricks and situations of a haunted house formula, with a murderous maniac on the loose, have been employed advantageously through god use of comedy effects. The 'Dead End Kids,' despite stereo routines, hang up a pretty good laugh score. Bela Lugosi, as the monster, here meets his match in the East Side hoodlums, or maybe it's vice versa.

Notes: Soon after the release of this film Donald Haines enlisted in the military.

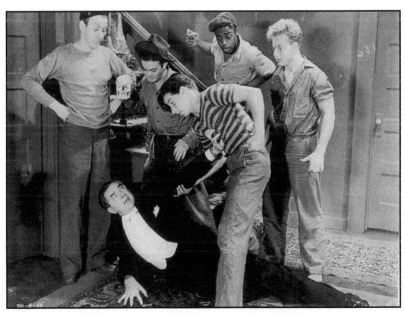

Hall, Gorcey, Jordan, Morrison, Haines trap Bela Lugosi

Mr. Wise Guy (Banner Production / Monogram, February 20, 1942)

Variety (March 4, 1942):

Monogram has reassembled the remnants of 'The Dead End Kids' (whom it bills 'The East Side Kids') for the umpteenth time and puts them into one of those reform school mellers which seem their perpetual destiny. It's no better, no worse, than all that have gone before and will slide into the same bottom-dual spot in the subsequent as its predecessor. The little rascals—pretty tiresome little rascals by now—are given new support in person of Billy Gilbert.

Notes: Gabriel Dell makes his first appearance with the kids in this film. Actor Bill Lawrence, in the part of Skinny, makes his one and only appearance as an East Side Kid.

Let's Get Tough (Banner Production / Monogram, May 22, 1942)

Variety (May 19, 1942):

Frustrated with their age which keeps the East Side toughies from serving in the Army; during World War 2 they wage a private war at home. Muggs and the gang first target a storekeeper whom they think to be Japanese, they pelt his store with rotten vegetables. When they enter the store they discover the owner has been stabbed to death. The kids are questioned and released by the police. Learning that the owner is actually Chinese, the gang makes a heartfelt apology to his widow. Plot of story is first rate and moves along fine with the direction from Wallace Fox…Gabriel Dell plays a convincing spy and makes his part work.

Notes: Sunshine Sammy Morrison's name was misspelled "Morrisson" in the onscreen credits.

Morrison, Gorcey, Lawrence, Jordan and Hall

Gorcey, Hall, Ann Doran, Billy Gilbert, David Gorcey, Jordan, Lawrence

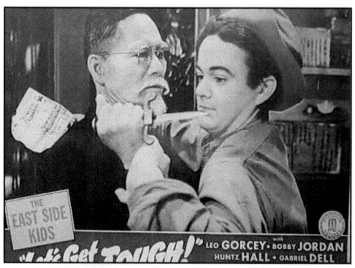

Lobby card for *Let's Get Tough*

Smart Alecks (Banner Production / Monogram, August 7, 1942)

Variety (September 2, 1942): *Smart Aleck's* a familiar yarn featuring the 'East Side Kids,' is an audience-pleaser despite the story, cast and production, which limit it to duals. The 'kids,' of course, are tough but with hearts of gold…Without the kids it's strictly sour stuff to digest. Especially good are Leo Gorcey, Huntz Hall and Sammy Morrison, the latter a Negro lad.

Clements, Gorcey and Jordan get the drop on Gabe Dell

Notes: David Gorcey entered the military after the completion of this film. Stanley Clements would make three films as a member of the East Side Kids; he would later become the leader of The Bowery Boys in the 1950s, when Leo Gorcey left the series.

Gabe Dell gets the point

'Neath Brooklyn Bridge (Banner Production / Monogram, November 20, 1942)

Variety (October 16, 1942):
　　The East Side Kids become unwittingly involved in a murder when they rescue Sylvia (Ann Gillis) from her abusive stepfather Morley, who is killed shortly thereafter by racketeer Marc Lawrence for stealing his money…Strictly for duals.

Clements, Ann Gillis, Morrison, Noah Beery, Jr., Hall, and Stone look

Kid Dynamite (Banner Production / Monogram, February 12, 1943)

Variety (February 17, 1943):
　　Tempo of the times saves this East Side Kid picture from being below mediocre. With the four leading characters going into the army, navy, and marines, the film sizes up passably for duals, particularly for those who have followed the antics of the toughies. Story, which appeared in the *Saturday Evening Post*, was written by Paul Ernst and apparently looked like a natural for the ex-Dead Enders. It's about a champion eastside kid boxer (Leo Gorcey) who is to box the westside champ…In addition to Gorcey, Hall and Jordan, Gabriel Dell turns in a stereotyped performance.

Notes: David Durand and Bennie Bartlett make their first appearances as East Side Kids. Wife Kay Marvis played the part of Leo Gorcey's dance partner Kay.

Clancy Street Boys (Banner Production / Monogram, April 23, 1943)

Variety (April 27, 1943):

Comedy element in 'Clancy Street Boys' makes it a fairly entertaining programmer aside from a plot that is somewhat unique for remnants of the Dead End Kids and other slum ruffians who are dubbed the East Side Kids in the picture. Should provide good support on double bills. In addition to the one gang headed by the wisecracking, smart-alecky Leo Gorcey, the story has made room for a rival bunch of tough young hoodlums who aid in providing action through free-for-all fights and the like.

Morrison, Bartlett, Durand, Gorcey, Stone and Hall

Notes: After the completion of his role of Stash, Dick Chandlee was drafted into the Army. Billy Benedict, Jimmy Strand and Johnny Duncan made their debuts in this entry as rival gang members, the Cherry Streeters.

Amelita Ward would later marry Leo Gorcey.

Bernard Gorcey, Leo and David's father, would later play the part of Louie Dumbrowski in the Bowery Boys film series. This was Eddie Mills' only appearance as an East Side Kid.

Eddie Mills, Jordan, Bartlett, Hall, Morrison, Noah Beery Sr., Gorcey,

Ghosts on the Loose (Banner Production / Monogram, July 30, 1943)

Variety (June 29, 1943):

Loosely constructed comedy thriller contains plenty of laughs despite the long procession of venerable gags. 'Ghost on the Loose' differs little from other East Side Kids epics, which means the mugs hog most of footage. Okay for supporting feature on twinners...Leo Gorcey, the little toughie leader of the kids, is tops, in the troupe, though mugging far too much. Huntz Hall, his No.1 stooge, is okay. Bobby Jordan and Billy Benedict also do well as other young mobsters.

Notes: In a scene in which actor Bela Lugosi sneezes, he sneezes out the words "oh shit"; director William Beaudine left the scene in the film.

This was Bobby Jordan's last film as a regular in the East Side Kids series; he entered the military. With this film Billy Benedict becomes an East Side Kid. Sunshine Sammy Morrison leaves the East Side Kid series.

Jordan, Hall, Bill Bates, Morrison, Gorcey, Stone, and Clements all look scared in this scene.

Mr. Muggs Steps Out (Banner Production / Monogram, October 29, 1943)

Variety (December 7, 1943):

The survivors of the original 'Dead End Kids' company, re-christened the 'East Side Kids' by Monogram, are served up in a corny comedy that should register with 'Kids' fan on a double bills. Leo Gorcey, titlerolist, is saved from a reform school term by Park Avenue matron Betty Blythe, whose hobby is to hire jailbirds as servants, thereby satisfying her social conscience and solving the servant problem…Repartee between Gorcey and Miss [Joan] Marsh is amusing, and manner in which Gorcey has gang do his dirty work nets laughs. Story itself is old stuff, but dialog and 'Kids' antics liven the proceedings. The original Dead-Enders—Gorcey, Huntz Hall and Gabriel Dell—are picking up too much weight and maturing much too rapidly to continue playing 'juve' delinquents. They look ripe for full-fledged gangster roles.

Notes: Jimmy Strand, Buddy Gorman and David Durand become members of the East Side Kids.

Nick Stuart and Joan Marsh help Leo Gorcey look for a dance partner

Million Dollar Kid (Banner Production / Monogram, February 28, 1944)

Variety (February 18, 1944):
Monogram's "East Side Kids" turn to the side of righteousness in their latest opus, giving an otherwise run-of-the-mill picture a fairly diverting twist. But, despite good direction by Wallace Fox, *Million Dollar Kid* will wind up on the lower rung in dual houses. Leo Gorcey, Huntz Hall and their cohorts rescue a wealthy man from a group of ruffians. He invites them to his home, where he explains that his son has become wayward. The boys decide to rid the neighborhood of ruffians, and find that the wealthy gent's son is one of the latter.

Herbert Heyes, Johnny Duncan, Gorcey, and Hall

Notes: This was Al Stone's (Herbert) only appearance in an East Side Kid film.

Gabe Dell winds up behind the eight ball.

Follow the Leader (Banner Production / Monogram, June 3, 1944)

Variety (May 30, 1944):

In tune with the times, the East Side Kids find "religion" and are on the side of law and order in *Follow the Leader*, which molds laughs and action into a fairly entertaining film. Story shows East Side Kids Leo Gorcey and Huntz Hall, on furlough from Army, conducting a private investigation (with military and police sanction) into a series of medical warehouse robberies...Gorcey, Hall, Gabriel Dell and Billy Benedict make a humorous foursome.

Notes: David Durand and Bobby Stone left the series to enter the military.

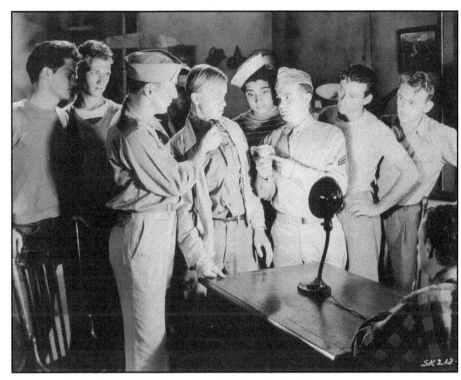

Scene from *Follow the Leader*

Gorcey and Dell both look bored in this scene

Block Busters (Banner Production / Monogram, July 22, 1944)

Variety (August 9, 1944):

This one spreads democracy thick on a thin plot. Another in the East Side Kids series, *Block Busters* is for lower half of duals. Film deals with antics of gang led by Leo Gorcey in taking into their midst a rich kid so he can learn the American way of life by associating with other boys. After making it almost unbearable for him, the East Side Kids realize the lad can stand up under their torments, and so he becomes one of them. Acting, direction and production values are lacking.

Gorcey and Hall play who's who

Bowery Champs (Banner Production / Monogram, November 25, 1944)

Variety (October 31, 1944):

The East Side Kids go reportorial in this one in tracking down a murder mystery. Although not always on even keel for a whodunit, it should do okay in the duals especially in spots where the kids retain b.o. hypo. Leo Gorcey is copyboy on newspaper and his pals work on delivery. A nitery owner is bumped off and Evelyn Brent, his ex-wife, is suspected.

Notes: Bobby Jordan was home on leave from the service and plays himself in this entry of the East Side Kids. This was Jimmy Strand's last film as an East Side Kid; he entered the military soon after its release.

Hall, Gorcey, and Dell are scolded by Minerva Urecal

Bobby Jordan makes his last appearance in this East Side film,
Bowery Champs

Docks of New York (Banner Production / Monogram, February 24, 1945)

Variety (February 24, 1945):

Latest in the East Side Kids series is better than average. Action is more involved and there's some amusing business. Pic is just fodder for the duals, of course, but it will do biz there. Story has the Kids—Muggs and Glimpy particularly—tied up in some knots concerning foreign agents, jewel thieves, murder and the law...Leo Gorcey, a little chubbier now, is still amusing and realistic as the little, tough Muggs, with Huntz Hall a good foil as his dopey stooge Glimpy.

Joy Reese, Gloria Pope, Pierre Watkin, and Betty Blythe stand by as they are questioned by Leo Gorcey about a valuable necklace.

Notes: Leo Borden, in the part of Peter, was only an East Side Kid for this film.

Leo Borden, Hall, Koenig, Gorcey, Gorman, and Benedict play
One Potato-Two Potato.

Mr. Muggs Rides Again (Banner Production / Monogram, July 15, 1945)

Variety (June 21, 1945):
The East Side Kids series takes a new lease on life in this film by transplanting the gang from city to country - to the racetrack, to be precise. Rough and tumble antics of Muggs, Glimpy, Danny and the others, plus some obvious humor, are dished up in an acceptable yarn to please ESK fans.

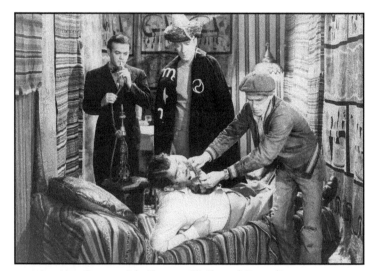
Scene with Gorcey, Hall, and Benedict.

Come Out Fighting (Banner Production / Monogram, September 29, 1945)

Variety (August 29, 1945):
"Come Out Fighting," 21 in the East Side Kid series, is entertainingly constructed and should provide a diverting hour as the supporting feature in duals. Pic deals with the police commissioner countermanding an order closing the gang's clubroom. Gang wants to show its appreciation by making a "man" out of his ballet-dancing son. Son gets involved with gamblers who are out to ruin his dad, at which point the kids come to the rescue. In addition to being the happy medium for Leo Gorcey, picture spotlights Mendie Koenig and Johnny Duncan, both do a fine job.

Gorcey, Duncan, Gorman, Koenig, Hall, and Benedict get good news from veterinarian Milton Kibbee.

Mendie Koenig and Billy Benedict give Gorcey their best shots

Live Wires (Monogram, January 12, 1946)

Variety (February 7, 1946):

Better production and featured casting values distinguish the first of the new Bowery Boys features from its predecessors, the East Side Kids series. These factors, plus the popularity enjoyed by the former series, give the replacement group excellent prospects in the Monogram market…Plot throws most of the emphasis to Gorcey, who's seen as a tough mug handy with his fists. Fisticuffs lose him one job after another, to the despair of his sister, until he lands with a process-serving outfit. This work fits his pugilistic tendencies and shapes story line for general roughhouse and broad comedy by the Bowery Boys…There's less mugging by Gorcey in this, but still sufficient to please his following. Major teamwork falls to Hall, leaving Bobby Jordan, Billy Benedict and a new mug, William Frambes, little to do except appear as atmosphere.

Lobby Card

Mike Mazurki

Slip waits to be slugged

In Fast Company (Monogram, June 22, 1946)

Variety (July 20, 1946):

Cavorting of Leo Gorcey and his Bowery Boys leaning but lightly on an unimportant and slight story feature Monogram's "In Fast Company." When viewed at the Brooklyn Strand, this comic-action opus garnered plenty of customer chuckles and knee-slapping. While not strong enough to carry on its own, as obligato to a bigger pic solid fare for the nabs. Plot serves its purpose by setting up comic situations which Gorcey and the boys exploit with gusto and copious corn. The story centers about the racketeering efforts of the manager of a large cab company to drive independents out of business…There's no scarcity of stock gags but, somehow the verve and dash which Gorcey and his gang inject into their efforts take the curse off the venerable lines. And Gorcey's lingo-mangling is still good for audience response.

Notes: David Gorcey plays the part of Chuck from this point on, in all the Bowery Boy films made. Bernard Gorcey makes his first appearance as Louie, owner of Louie's Sweet Shop.

Belgium one sheet

Benedict, Gorcey, Frank Marlowe, Paul Harvey, Jane Randolph, Jordan,
Paul Harvey wanting some answers

Bowery Bombshell (Monogram, July 20, 1946)

Variety (July 16, 1946):
Standard entry in Monogram's "Bowery Boys" series will sell in its intended market. Stock plot is sparked by Leo Gorcey's mugging antics...Rowdy action stems from fact that one of the boys is mistaken for a bank robber and bunch sets out to trap real crooks so Huntz Hall can be cleared.

Benedict, Jordan, David Gorcey, William "Wee" Willie Davis

Leo Gorcey and Teala Loring

Spook Busters (Monogram, August 24, 1946)

Variety (August 20, 1946):

Film comedy, nurtured on slapstick, reverts to early childhood in "Spook Busters." Entire story, with all its attendant comedy business, reeks of gleanings from past productions long gone into the limbo of unremembered celluloid. There is the ever-present feeling of having seen all this somewhere before. And yet spotty as the screen values are there are a lot of laughs among the hokum. Even the old business of two people, searching for something in a wall, and answering each other's knocks, is used. Overall, however, the film drags and is repetitious. It hasn't much appeal except to grammar school level and weekend matinee business.

Notes: Gabe Dell makes his first entry in a Bowery Boy film.

The Bowery Boys graduate from insect exterminator college.

Benedict, Hall, Jordan, Leo and David Gorcey

Mr. Hex (Monogram, December 7, 1946)

Variety (December 4, 1946):

"Mr. Hex" settles into the Bowery Boys series grove capably, furnishing plenty of antics liked by those who follow the doings of the rough-and-ready gang. Original story uses novel gimmick to spark chuckles, and production values furnished by Jan Grippo get the most from budget expenditure. Story pattern is developed around hypnotism, a device used by the Boweryites for their latest do-good action…Leo Gorcey, as gang leader, learns trick of hypnotizing Huntz Hall into believing he's strong as 10 men. Boys pit Hall in an amateur boxing contest in a try for prize money and through slapdash adventures they make the payoff…Film spots a number of surefire laugh touches such as gamblers employing an "evil-eye" character to counter-hex Hall and pickpocket to snatch Gorcey's hypnotizing coin.

Danny Beck, David Gorcey, Leo Gorcey, and a crying Hall, and Jordan.

Leo Gorcey, David Gorcey, Bernard Gorcey (hidden), Hall, Jordan, Benedict

Hard Boiled Mahoney (Monogram, April 26, 1947)

Variety (April 8, 1947)

"Hard Boiled Mahoney" strives hard for laughs with worn out clichés, slapstick comedy and ungrammatical English. Entire cast plays "straight" for Leo Gorcey who takes over as an amateur detective. Half the plot is solved while other part is left to audience detective's imagination. Film will, nevertheless, hold up with a strong mate…Gorcey indulges in his usual murder of the English language which some regard as amusing. Huntz Hall wears a funny hat. Bobby Jordan, Gabriel Dell, Billy Benedict and David Gorcey complete the mob that hangs out in the soda fountain run by Bernard Gorcey.

Gorcey and Hall come up short against Noble Johnson

Poster for *News Hounds*

News Hounds (Monogram, August 13, 1947)

Variety (June 11, 1947):

"News Hounds" adds up to one of the best of Monogram's Bowery Boys series. Playoff will be good in the market for which it's aimed. As title indicates, it's a newspaper story with Leo Gorcey as ambitious copyboy. Jan Grippo's production has given boys a plot to work over and that accounts for more substance than usually found in B.B. entries. Gorcey wants to be a star reporter and around his efforts in that direction the antics are built… Gorcey continues his garbled-word way for chuckles; his antics pleasing. Huntz Hall, Gorcey's dopey pal, backs up the fun strongly.

Publicity still with Anthony Caruso, Leo Gorcey and Christine McIntyre

Bowery Buckaroos (Monogram, November 22, 1947)

Variety (October 7, 1947):

Lampooning the oaters, this low budgeter hands the Bowery Boys free rein to lead their horses from New York's East Side water holes to the wild and wooly west. In changing their stamping grounds from the metropolis to the mesa, the boys dish out plenty of zanyisms charged with uninhibited corn, but the less discriminating filmgoer will find plenty of laughs in their antics. Picture should do well in the nabes - especially with the juve trade. Plot is an inconsequential one of those things. But who cares when Leo Gorcey is getting off such gems of idiom as, "I'm goin' out and prosecute for gold." Scripters Tim Ryan and Edmond Seward pitched plenty of grist into the gag mill. Even an Indian comes up with incongruous lingo, e.g., his analysis of a peculiar situation, "This don't look kosher to me!"

Notes: This film marked the end of Bobby Jordan's stint as one of the Bowery Boys.

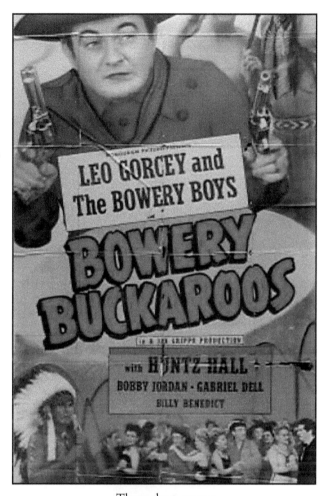

Three-sheet poster

Bowery Boys arrive in the old west

Angels' Alley (Monogram, March 21, 1948)

Variety (January 14, 1948):

"Angels' Alley" measures up as okay comedy-melodrama for the Bowery Boys' fans. Sparked by Leo Gorcey and Huntz Hall, the antics fit into the accepted pattern for the series and returns should stack up with others in the group. This time Gorcey turns his attention to busting up a car-stealing ring that is making bad boys out of his sidewalk buddies. Script has an occasional sparkle and plotting is good. Besides the comedy mugging of Gorcey and Hall, there's a serious moment thrown in now and then, and William Beaudine's direction keeps it all moving for fast 67 minutes.

Poster for *Angels' Alley*

Benedict, Nestor Paiva, and Gorcey all look perplexed

Jinx Money (Monogram, June 27, 1948)

Variety (May 12, 1948):

"Jinx Money" is an easily salable Bowery Boys entry from Monogram stable. Strictly for laughs, it has a slap-happy pace calculated to please any following built by the series, and pay-off in that particular market will be good. Plot combines comedy and melodrama effectively enough to show off the antics of the Bowery Boys led by Leo Gorcey. Direction by William Beaudine paces the chuckles and thrills for best all-around reception, letting the Bowery gang have its head in frantic antics—a formula particularly pleasing to series fans. A gambler wins $50.000 at cards and is murdered on the street while carrying away the loot. Gorcey and Hall find it and the fun develops in their trying to keep it against the onslaught of other gamblers and a killer. Boys out-trick the brains at every turn and there are five murders before the killer is brought to justice.

Notes: Bennie Bartlett becomes a member of the Bowery Boys, playing the part of Butch.

Publicity still for *Jinx Money* with David Gorcey, Benedict, Sheldon Leonard, Leo Gorcey, and Bennie Bartlett

Scene from *Jinx Money*

Smugglers' Cove (Monogram, October 24, 1948)

Variety (October 16, 1948):

Leo Gorcey and Huntz Hall are at it again in another of their English-murdering minor epics. Results guarantee pleasure of followers - and those not too familiar with the slapstick derring-do staged by Monogram's tough kids. As a secondary, particularly in the action market, it's good material. "Smugglers Cove" is a loosely-knit scramble of malapropos and adventure. It starts when Gorcey mistakenly receives letter notifying him of

Slip prepares to hit Count Petrov Bons with a chair.

the inheritance of a Long Island estate. He and his gang trek to the manor, find it occupied by a gang smuggling aliens into the country...The rough, but noble of heart characters fit Gorcey, Hall, Gabriel Dell, Billy Benedict, David Gorcey and Bennie Bartlett like gloves and they wear them with swaggering aplomb.

Publicity still for *Smugglers' Cove* with Martin Kosleck, Eddie Gribbon, Gorcey and Hall

Trouble Makers (Monogram, December 10, 1948)

Variety (December 16, 1948):
"Trouble Makers" is a better than average Bowery Boys cutup from Monogram studio. A whodunit with comedy neatly scripted to please in the series regular market. It will have no trouble making its way among the general situations. Leo Gorcey and Huntz Hall are the prime trouble-makers, playing their lead roles a bit straighter than usual. Pair operates a sidewalk telescope business and when they witness a murder in a hotel blocks away their troubles commence. They enlist a cop friend to help smoke out the mystery. There are frame-ups; gambling raids and the menace of gang murder always present to keep suspense backing the comedy deliveries before Gorcey, Hall and cop pal Gabriel Dell clean up the mystery. Two leads' antics are perfectly tuned to please their fans and others will find plenty to chuckle at, too…Jan Grippo's production supervision ably realizes on necessary values to put this one over, and Reginald LeBorg's direction gives the script a snappy pace.

(left to right) Hall, Lionel Stander, John Indrisano, Gorcey, John Ridgely and Frankie Darro

The boys play rough in this scene with Lionel Stander.

Fighting Fools (Monogram, April 17, 1949)

Variety (April 19, 1949):

"Fighting Fools" is a moderately entertaining programmer with a prize fight background. Although there are liberal fight scenes, these sequences for the most part are pegs on which to hang the crusty humor of the Bowery Boys, who are ring mastered by Leo Gorcey. Film rates as average supporting material...Gorcey and his Bowery Boy colleagues -

Slip and Johnny Higgins face boxing commission

Huntz Hall, Gabriel Dell, et al, breeze through their roles to generate as many laughs as possible. Plot itself takes a secondary spot to their antics.

Notes: This was the only Bowery Boy film that former East Side Kid Johnny Duncan would appear in.

Slip, Chuck, Johnny Higgins, Butch, Whitey and Sach receive a call from
the boxing commission

Hold That Baby! (Monogram, June 26, 1949)

Variety (June 18, 1949):
Jan Grippo's newest entry for the Bowery Boys, "Hold That Baby," should be "Hold That Script." Boys are operators of a Laundromat; they find a baby in a linen basket. The infant is Jonathan Andrews III, heir to very large fortune…Plot is weak, but cast has a few stand outs.

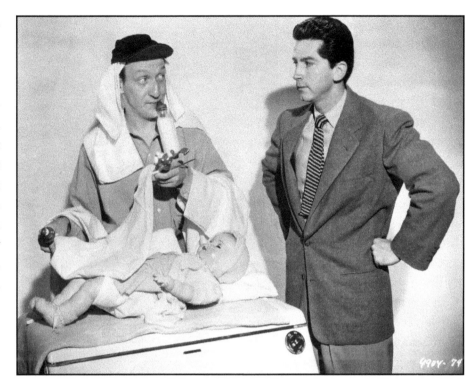

Angels in Disguise (Monogram, September 11, 1949)

Variety (September 10, 1949):
Hollywood's first attempt at a comic documentary comes up aces in "Angels in Disguise." Latest in the Bowery Boys series is a credit to all concerned. Film will be a howl in the sticks and draw plenty of chuckles when paired with a biggie in key city first-runs. Film has drawn a neat screenplay, credit from Charles R Marion, Gerald Schnitzer and Bert Lawrence. Idea of doing a series film as a documentary in a light vein is a new and smart one. It is one which will pay off and create plenty of new fans for the series. Dialogue, also is topnotch. Plot itself, however, is a slight one in just six words; Bowery Boys help police catch killers. It is the way film is done that makes it rise above the ordinary.

Notes: Pepe Hern (Bertie Spangler) told me. "Gorcey was a very generous guy; he always took the cast to lunch after filming to the famous Brown Derby restaurant. There were two hangouts

Publicity still with Gorcey, Hall, and Mickey Knox

Someone's going to get hurt here. Hall, Joe Turkel, Mickey Knox and Pepe Hern

in Hollywood for actors. One was Schwab's and the other was Café de Paris on Sunset and Vine, we all met up there on various occasions. We would get together with the likes of Howard Keel, Peggy Lee, John Carradine and directors like Anthony Mann. Leo and his non-acting friends made it a lively place. Huntz Hall was a character, always joking around. A very funny guy."

Master Minds (Monogram, November 20, 1949)

Variety (December 27, 1949):

As the latest in Monogram's Bowery Boys series, "Master Minds" fails to measure up to the quality of some of its predecessors. Thin plot brings off a flock of trite situations in which Leo Gorcey, Huntz Hall and rest flounder around for meager results. Film's market will be limited to the lower half of the duals. Gorcey occasionally gives the picture a lift with his familiar grammatical distortions of the

Publicity still with Jane Adams, Glenn Strange, and Gorcey

spoken word, but neither his thesping nor that of his supporting players is strong enough to offset the clichéd yarn of Charles R. Marion.

Alan Napier, Glenn Strange and Hall

Blonde Dynamite (Monogram, February 12, 1950)

Variety (February 21, 1950):

"Blonde Dynamite," latest in Jan Grippo's "Bowery Boys" series, shapes up as passable fare for the lesser twin-billers. Comedy and the situations of the Charles Marion script are rather forced, but nevertheless achieve frequent chuckles. Script hands Leo Gorcey his familiar ungrammatical lines and he makes the most of them for maximum effect. Joining the general buffoonery are Gorcey's cohorts - Huntz Hall, Gabriel Dell, and William Benedict. Laughs get underway when the group converts Bernard Gorcey's ice-cream parlor into an escort bureau…Brash and earthily amusing Gorcey moves through his role with a minimum of effort, although giving the film a pulchritudinous lift.

Notes: Buddy Gorman takes over the role of Butch from Bennie Bartlett.

Hall surrounded by beauties (left) Karen Randle and Beverlee Crane

Louie Dumbrowski, Mrs. Dumbrowski (Jody Gilbert) and Slip

Lucky Losers (Monogram, May 14, 1950)

Variety (May 26, 1950):

Jan Grippo's "Bowery Boys" series gets a shot in the arm with "Lucky Losers," which continues the exploits of Leo Gorcey and Huntz Hall. Current film carries a sounder plot than majority of series' offerings, and stacks up as a go-getting second feature, lending itself particularly well to exploitation…there's plenty of comedy, of the particular brand proffered by Gorcey and Hall, and melodrama, both combining to build up legitimate plot. Gorcey handles his role in his customary efficient fashion, but should drop a bit of his weight. Hall, too, delivers in his usual broad style.

Triple Trouble (Monogram, August 13, 1950)

Variety (September 5, 1950):

Another in the Bowery Boys series, "Triple Trouble" is a routine entry for the dualer situations. Formula is pat, with gang finding itself up to its ears in trouble which it eventually irons out. Film sports the usual quota of yock material conveyed via corny actions and lines. Leo Gorcey is on hand to chieftain the boys and murder the King's English with his constant misuse of words, one of the angles used mostly to draw laughs. Huntz Hall, as Gorcey's No. 1 stooge, continues to take the brunt of friendly insults and abuse dished out by the latter. Rest of the gang, made up of Billy Benedict, Buddy Gorman and David Gorcey, have little to do…Gorcey gives his role the characterization it demands, mugging throughout, while Hall does a convincing job as his exasperating buddy.

Butch, Whitey, Chuck, Sach and Slip wanting free banana splits

Bat Armstrong and unidentified actor want the lowdown

Lyn Thomas tries her best in this game of Who's Who.

Blues Busters (Monogram, October 29, 1950)

Variety (October 19, 1950):

Monogram's Bowery Boys have a somewhat different entry. In "Blues Busters," they take to song to bolster the usual pattern of rowdy mugging, and it all comes off successfully for their market. It's a good twist for this standard series. When Huntz Hall suddenly develops a golden crooning voice after a tonsillectomy, Leo Gorcey, the Bowery mastermind, sees it as an opportunity to become rich…Producer Jan Grippo gives the picture a smarter looking mounting than entries in the series are usually accorded. Casting also is good for laugh and release intentions. Gorcey is his expected self as the brash kingpin of the Bowery group. Syncing of Hall's mugging to offstage singing of John Lorenz is very good, and the piping is an able assist in selling the song catalog.

Notes: This was Gabriel Dell's last film as one of the Bowery Boys; he left the series to perform on the New York stage in the play *Tickets Please* (1950)

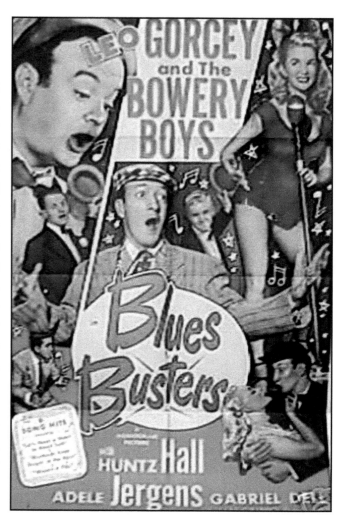

Craig Stevens, Adele Jergens and Gorcey

Bowery Battalion (Monogram, January 24, 1951)

Variety (February 7, 1951):

Monogram may have a sleeper in this Jan Grippo production of the Bowery Boys series. Produced, budget-wise, for dual houses, pic could well carry top side of a twin bill and might even stand alone and do business. Film gets in on top of cycle of army camp comedies which is sure to come in view of mobilization. Loaded with gags, some familiar and some new.

Publicity still of Leo Gorcey. Notice him wearing a wedding ring

Ghost Chasers (Monogram, April 29, 1951)

Variety (May 23, 1951):

Monogram's latest entry in the Bowery Boy series is no better or worse than past episodes and should do okay as a lower dualer. As "Ghost Chasers," the boys go into action to smash a phoney spiritualist ring with daring and zany comedics that should please...Gorcey, as the Bowery Boys chief, continues murdering the King's English and badgering his aides and his enemies with over-eager fists. Hall complements him adequately as the "moron" Bowery member, and Lloyd Corrigan adds a fey touch to the proceedings as the 300-year-old ghost.

Slip pleading his case to Cynthia [Jan Kayne]

Let's Go Navy! (Monogram, July 29, 1951)

Variety (July 26, 1951):

"Let's Go Navy," 23d in the Bowery Boys series, hits a high entertainment niche. It's bright comedy throughout and ranks tops for the supporting market. The fine script by Max Adams provides a neat foil for the comedy antics of the "boys." The lines are bright; the routines tops, though the plot itself is actually thin.

Notes: *Let's Go Navy!* was the last film produced by Jan Grippo. This was also the last film for Buddy Gorman, as Butch, one of the Bowery Boys; he was replaced by Bennie Bartlett, who, for the next 17 films, played the part until he retired from films in 1956.

Gorcey and Charlita do the hula

The Bowery Boys watch Charlita do her dance

Crazy Over Horses (Monogram, November 18, 1951)

Variety (**November 21, 1951**):

Leo Gorcey and some other former "Dead End Kids" (now dubbed the Bowery Boys) are not as funny as they used to be. But it is not so much their fault as that of the director and scripter. They sound like their old selves when given a chance in this screwball comedy, but that's not often enough... *Crazy Over Horses* tries to stretch a routine comedy idea into a racetrack feature. Idea of the Bowery Boys being handed possession of a racehorse in payment for a food bill, finally making a killing with the mount in a big race, is not exactly new...Gorcey, still the boy gang leader, gets laughs, as usual, surmounting some of the more inane moments. Bernard Gorcey makes something of the store proprietor.

Notes: This was Billy Benedict's last film as one of the Bowery Boys.

Benedict, Hall, Gorcey, Gloria Saunders, Bernard Gorcey and David Gorcey

Slip plays "I got your nose" with Sach and guard Bob Peoples

Hold That Line (Monogram, March 23, 1952)

Variety (March 25, 1952):

Slapstick and uninhibited comedy, which have marked Monogram's Bowery Boys series since its inception, again get a work over in "Hold That Line." Humor is of the obvious type. However, this entry will qualify as supporting fare for the duals where exhibs are seeking something with a light touch to balance off heavy drama. At the behest of two alumni, the Bowery Boys (Leo Gorcey, Huntz Hall et al.) enroll as students in an Ivy League college. Old grads are testing a theory that they can transform uncouth boys into shining examples of culture…Monogram has a good series in the Bowery Boys. However, each entry is only as good as its material, and future releases will have to come up with fresher situations and fun making if they're to retain their following. Leo Gorcey, Hall and their cohorts do the best they can for fair results.

Sach gets a kiss from leading lady (Mona Knox) Katie Wayne

Here Come the Marines (Monogram, June 29, 1952)

Variety (May 21, 1952):

A mildly diverting programmer in Monogram's low-budget Bowery Boys series. Leo Gorcey, Huntz Hall and their Bowery henchmen this time find themselves in the Marines. Hall, through a fluke (the

The boys with Myrna Dell.

colonel knew his father), is made a sergeant, and as a whistle-happy, sad-sack non-com makes the training life of his friends thoroughly miserable…A change in command leads to Hall's demotion and Gorcey takes over the sergeant's stripes. Characterization of Gorcey, Hall and the other Bowery Boys are familiar.

Feudin' Fools (Monogram, September 21, 1952)

Variety (September 19, 1952):

Latest in Monogram's "Bowery Boys" entry holds up just fine, designed to fit into their mold. "Feudin' Fools" comes off hokey at times but is sure to please their fans. "Sach," Huntz Hall, discovers he is heir to a country farm in hillbilly land, and he and the boys set out to claim his cows and chicks. Hall does some milking and chicken feeding for some comic effect. While on the farm, they learn that the "Jones" name is not too popular, as the neighboring Smiths are having a feud with the Joneses'. Leo Gorcey and Huntz Hall are excellent with their mugging, but pic belongs to Hall.

Scene from *Feudin' Fools*

No Holds Barred (Monogram, November 23, 1952)

Variety (December 17, 1952):

Latest in Monogram's "Bowery Boys" entries stacks up as a good programmer designed to fit smoothly into the lower half of duals, slot for which this production is geared. "No Holds Barred" stars Leo Gorcey, with Huntz Hall as his foil, and should find favor with exhibs in its particular niche. Plot hangs on Hall's strange physical insensitivity which makes him immune to feeling. Gorcey capitalizes on this, turning it into a business advantage by converting Hall into a rassler, and Hall wins by using his head—to knock out his opponents…Scrambled verbiage which has served Gorcey so well through the years comes off well, but he should do something about the additional avoirdupois he's been adding lately. Hall is excellent with his mugging and language mutilation.

There's no subtlety in the ribbing of rassling, and broad ring scenes fit into the general tenor of the production.

Notes: This was the last Bowery Boy film made for the Monogram name; the company henceforth became known as Allied Artists.

Jalopy (Allied Artists, February 15, 1953)

Variety (March 20, 1953):

"Jalopy," latest in Allied Artists Bowery Boys series, is on the level of its recent predecessors, an above-par programmer. Premise of mixing Leo Gorcey and Huntz Hall with a jalopy-racing backdrop is a good one, and the boys do it justice, drawing out the chuckles. Screenplay by Tim Ryan and Jack Crutcher, with some additional dialog by Bert Lawrence, serves mainly to allow Gorcey to continue his murderous use of the English language and Hall to prove himself a complete wack.

Lobby card from *Jalopy* with Gorcey, Jane Easton and Hall

Scene with Murray Alper, Richard Benedict, Robert Lowery, Hall, Leon Belasco, Gorcey, David Gorcey, and Bartlett

Loose in London (Allied Artists, May 24, 1953)

Variety (June 26, 1953):

"Loose in London" entry, which shifts the scene from New York to London for the unfoldment of its zany comedians, the Bowery Boys, is worthwhile. Good use is made of London backgrounds for production values, and situations and gags are fashioned around setting to keep regular audiences satisfied...Hall walks away with the honors here, some of his clowning drawing belly laughs from series' addicts. Gorcey is in there with his usual malapropisms, and Bernard Gorcey, in the role of sweet shop operator who goes along, is his frantic self despite having less to do than usual.

Scene with Clyde Cook, Bernard, Gorcey, Leo, and Hall

Publicity still. Gorcey gets a kiss from Angela Greene

Clipped Wings (Allied Artists, August 14, 1953)

Variety (November 20, 1953):

Latest entry in the "Bowery Boys" series fits neatly into the accepted formula and should rack up satisfactory returns in program's regular market. Yarn's U.S. Air Force background gives the familiar characters of Leo Gorcey and Huntz Hall opportunity to play out their customary brand of nonsensical shenanigans…Gorcey and Hall contribute their usual fast-paced characterizations, latter taking the lead over Gorcey, under Edward Bernds' know-how direction.

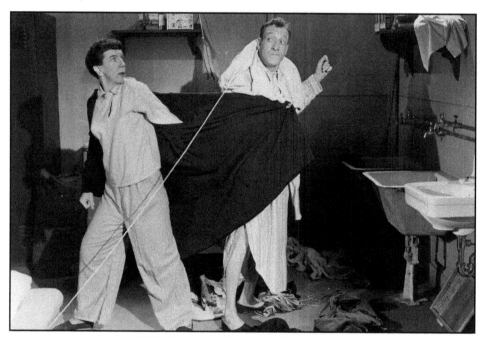

Hall plays tug-of-war with Renie Riano

Sgt. Bronsky (Henry Kulky) serves Sach a banana split

Publicity still of Hall

Private Eyes (Allied Artists, December 6, 1953)

Variety (November 28, 1953):
"Sach" of the "Bowery Boys" becomes a mind-reader in this latest entry from Allied Artists, and should do well at the box office…There are some funny moments in pic. "Sach" predicts what the envelope holds, and the blowing up of a safe. Gorcey with his malapropos and Hall's craziness makes film enjoyable.

Professor Sach cooks up a rocket formula.

Paris Playboys (Allied Artists, March 7, 1954)

Variety (March 5, 1954)
The Bowery Boys become "Paris Playboys" for this latest in their Allied Artists series. It's not up to its predecessors, yet adequate supporting fare. The laughs don't come frequently nor with ease in the script dished up by Elwood Ullman and Edward Bernds. Main springboards, per usual, are the malapropos of Leo Gorcey and Huntz Hall's crazy antics… Bernard Gorcey is okay and, as the pint-sized side-kick of the Boys, impersonates Toulouse-Lautrec in one brief scene for the film's cleverest bit.

Bernard and Leo share a moment

The Bowery Boys Meet the Monsters (Allied Artists, June 6, 1954)

Variety (June 30, 1954):

"The Bowery Boys Meet the Monsters" goes overboard on the malapropisms which generally give zest to series in this latest release of Allied Artists' bread-and-butter program. The Ben Schwalb production is on the weak side, not up to the usual standard, with appeal even for followers of the series apt to be limited. This time, Leo Gorcey and Huntz Hall, in their familiar zany characters, get involved in a household of madmen seeking to obtain human heads for their scientific experiments. One wants a brain with a low I.Q. for transference to the skull of a giant ape, another a head to attach to an electronic robot, controlled, by a microphone.

Slip and Gorog the Robot (Norman Bishop)

Jungle Gents (Allied Artists, September 5, 1954)

Variety (September 7, 1954):

The "Bowery Boys" in Africa is the latest from Allied Artists in the Bowery Boy series. "Sach," who has sinus trouble, takes medication which increases his sense of smell. Diamonds are found with the other boys when they travel to Africa, and expose a fake spirit, scaring the natives. They encounter bad guys, Goebel and Shanks (Rudolph Anders, Harry Cording), who plan to steal diamonds, when the nose of Hall finds them.

Gorcey outsmarts tough guys, while Hall plays kiss-kiss with jungle girl Laurette Luez.

Not much of a plot and stock footage doesn't help matters any, neither the narration from Gorcey. Screenplay by Elwood Ullman and director Edward Bernds is below-par for both.

Pressbook for *Jungle Gents*

Bowery to Bagdad (Allied Artists, January 2, 1955)

Variety (January 3, 1955):

    Story line for this latest Bowery Boy entry has the boys in Bagdad, after reading newspaper of a missing lamp. Sach finds and buys said lamp, and the fun begins…Director Edward Bernds makes this screenplay from Elwood Ullman and he work to the boy's advantage.

Hall, Gorcey, and Joan Shawlee

High Society (Allied Artists, April 17, 1955)

Variety (April 26, 1955):

High Jinks in high society by Leo Gorcey and Huntz Hall feature this run-of-the-mill entry in a routine, so-called bread-and-butter comedy series. Like most of its predecessors, "High Society" exhibits little pride in the profession of filmmaking, but as a flat rental offering for dualers it fulfills release intentions...Around that shell a lot of typical Gorcey-Hall nonsense has been padded in the scripting by Bert Lawrence and Jerome S. Gottler from a story by Edward Bernds and Elwood Ullman.

Spy Chasers (Allied Artists, July 31, 1955)

Variety (October 2, 1955):

The Bowery Boys are "Spy Chasers" in this latest entry, dishing out their usual slapstick comedy in par for the course. Screenplay by Bert Lawrence and Jerome S. Gottler provides Leo Gorcey and Huntz Hall, stars of the series, the ingredients for their favorite pastimes - hitting each other over the head or making with malapropos...With 38 previous "BB" features under their belt, Gorcey and Hall have long mastered their respective roles in manner pleasing to followers of the series.

Gorcey and Hall

How many licks to the center?

Jail Busters (Allied Artists, September 18, 1955)

Variety (September 21, 1955):
The newest "Bowery Boy entry "Jail Busters" is sharp and sure to please the following of their antics. Newspaper employee Chuck working undercover for a paper suffers a beating while doing a story in prison on corruption. Leo Gorcey and pals get themselves sent up to the Big House, for a robbery, with the help from Chuck's newspaper editor...Prison scenes are standard, but mug shot scenes make up for any laps in funniness.

Slip is questioned by Cy Bowman (Lyle Talbot)

Scene from *Jail Busters*

Dig That Uranium (Allied Artists, January 8, 1956)

Variety (February 16, 1956):

The laughs come only spasmodically in "Dig That Uranium," with result that this 40th entry in Allied Artists' Bowery Boys series at best shapes as filler fare. In whipping up the screenplay, Elwood Ullman and Bert Lawrence seemed to have concentrated to a greater extent on Leo Gorcey's malapropos than on a story line upon which to hang some good comedic situations…Gorcey and Huntz Hall, also starred, cavort again in the same manner which seemingly has pleased followers of this series for years, pair having long ago mastered their respective roles.

Notes: Bernard Gorcey, the lovable Louie Dumbrowski, was involved in an auto accident on August 31, 1955. He died eleven days later, on September 11, 1955.

Bennie Bartlett also left the Bowery Boy film series at this time.

The boys encounter Indians while looking for uranium

Crashing Las Vegas (Allied Artists, April 22, 1956)

Variety (April 17, 1956): "Crashing Las Vegas" may not be the best in this long series of "Bowery Boy" films, but has plenty of laughs. After receiving an electric jolt Huntz Hall is able to predict numbers and wins a night stay in Las Vegas after appearing on a game show. Gangsters watch every move as he wins with every spin at a roulette table…This is Hall's film all the way, and Leo Gorcey is just shadow dressing.

Notes: This was Leo Gorcey's last Bowery Boy film. It has been rumored that after finishing his last scenes for this film, Leo threw a chair which hit Huntz Hall and cried, "Papa! Please come back!" In my lengthy conversations with David Gorcey and Huntz Hall, they both told me that this story was untrue. David simply stated that it was "pure shit." Hall said it was "a fucking lie!" However, it was true that Leo had to be driven home from the set due to his drinking.

Stanley Cements would, after this film, take over the helm as the leader of the Bowery Boys, in the role of Stanislaus 'Duke' Coveleske. Jimmy Murphy (Myron) became one of the Bowery Boys in this film.

Scene with Hall, Gorcey, David Gorcey and Jimmy Murphy

Murphy, David Gorcey, Leo and Huntz meet in the execution chamber with Frank Hagney

Fighting Trouble (Allied Artists, September 16, 1956)

Variety (September 12, 1956):
Huntz Hall, now in the lead role as the head of the Bowery Boys, aided by Stanley Clements in this latest entry from Allied Artists. "Fighting Trouble" is a little pic that should do well on under bills.

Hot Shots (Allied Artists, December 23, 1956)

Variety (December 3, 1956):
"Hot Shots," the latest in the long running Bowery Boy series, is not at the top of the ladder. Sach and Duke find themselves the baby sitter of an eight-year-old TV star, after the kid steals their car. The executives, who think the boys know how to handle the boy, hired them to watch over him…The laughs are slow in coming, which make for a dull afternoon.

Queenie Smith gives Clements and Hall a tug

Hold That Hypnotist (Allied Artists, February 24, 1957)

Variety (March 10, 1957):
Allied Artists' "Hold That Hypnotist" is the latest Bowery Boy film, starring long nose wacky Huntz Hall and Stanley Clements. Hall is hypnotized in an effort to uncover a quack hypnotist, who transplants him to the year 1682, when he lived a previous life as a tax collector who has won a treasure map once belonging to Blackbeard the Pirate.

Spook Chasers (Allied Artists, June 2, 1957)

Variety (July 12, 1957):
    "Spook Chasers," the latest Bowery Boy feature, might have done well at the box office if released later in the year, say October, for the little ones. Boys, Huntz Hall, Stanley Clements and the rest, go to a mountain cabin to help fellow friend Mike try and rest his tired nerves.

    Notes: Eddie LeRoy (Blinky) makes his first appearance in this Bowery Boy film.

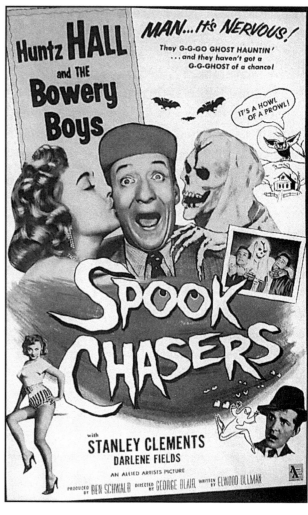

Publicity still

Looking for Danger (Allied Artists, October 6, 1957)

Variety (November 3, 1957):
    This may be the weakest Bowery Boy entry from Allied Artists to date. Plot centers around "Duke," the leader of the boys, telling an officer for the War Department how he and the boys lost a pop during the War. There are dancing girls in the retelling of how the boys were sent on a mission to locate "The Hawk," a member of the underground.

    Notes: Jimmy Murphy left the series; he had made five films as one of the Bowery Boys.

Up in Smoke (Allied Artists, December 22, 1957)

Variety (December 18, 1957):

Latest saga of the Bowery Boy series "Up in Smoke" has Hall selling his soul to the devil (Byron Foulger) for horse racing tips, so that he can put charity funds back that he lost…Director William Beaudine might have been nodding a little on this one.

In the Money (Allied Artists, February 16, 1958)

Variety (March 11, 1958):

This may well be the last Bowery Boy pic made for Allied Artists, if one reads the trades. Huntz Hall is hired by jewel thieves to chaperone a poodle on a cross-country cruise to London. His employers have hidden jewels in the dog's coat, to go undetected by Scotland Yard, who are close behind. "Duke" and the boys stowaway on the ship to keep "Sach" out of trouble…On the directing side of this yawn is William Beaudine, who has done better. Screenplay by Al Martin and story by Elwood Ullman could have made this one fun, with a little more laughs.

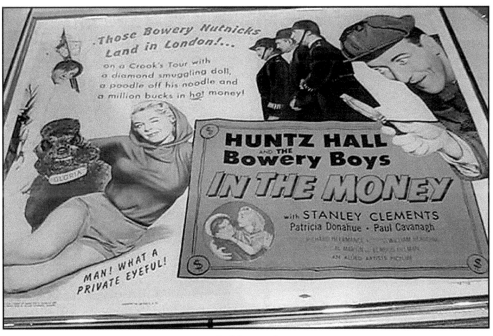

Lobby card

Revivals

Since the original play *Dead End* opened on Broadway on October 28, 1935, there have been three successful revivals.

The first one opened on April 25, 1978, at the Quaigh Theater, located in the Diplomat Hotel in New York. It was directed by Will Lieberson. On this special night the cast members were greeted with a standing ovation led by Sidney Kingsley, who was the writer and director of the original Broadway production.

In the Dead End Kid roles were Michael Stumm, as T.B.; Fred Ivory as Angel; Craig Alfano as Dippy; Peter Jeffrries Ferrara as Spit and Hal Muchnick as Tommy. A review of the play from the *New York Times*, on May 5, 1978, stated that the "seems a little dated, but the kids seem new. The six young actors are filled with energy and cockiness, something that has not been seen in sometime. Of the six actors, Peter Jeffries Ferrara stands out in the role of Spit—shades of Leo Gorcey. One understands why the Dead End Kids were to evolve from this play."

In 2005, the play was performed again, at the Los Angeles Ahmanson Theatre, by the Center Theatre Group. Artistic Director Michael Ritchie, a self-proclaimed Dead End Kids fan, undertook this revival. This production from Ritchie would be his third, with the first two being in 1997 (Williamstown Theatre Festival in Berkshires, Massachusetts) and again in 2000 (Huntington Theatre in Boston).

The elaborate setting at the Ahmanson Theatre had something that the original Belasco production did not have: real water. The orchestra pit was lined with a black pool liner, to simulate New York's East River. Eleven thousand gallons of water, from the Los Angeles Fire Department, were used to fill the lined pit. This added to the realism when the kid actors had to do their splashes and swimming.

With a budget of well over $3,000, the man behind creating the 48-foot tenement sets and the East River was James Noone. Lights had to be mounted to the ceilings so that a worker could move along with cast members to stay in focus.

Director Nicholas Martin, who had been with Ritchie for his earlier productions, made the whole play come together. Seated in the audience on a Sunday afternoon in October of 2005 were Leo Gorcey, Jr. Gabriel Dell, Jr. Bobby Jordan, Jr. and the nieces and nephews of Billy Halop, and author Len Getz, who were greeted by cast members after their performance.

The third and final revival of the play *Dead End* took place in Chicago, Illinois, at the Griffin Theatre, running for a period of 43 days, October 1 2006-November 12, 2006.

A review in the *Chicago Sun-Times*, on October 3, 2006, said, "A Depression-era classic…is sure to please. Sure, it has its antique aspects, but director Jonathan Berry's period-perfect staging and fine ensemble work of his 27 actors keep you engaged. Berry has done a great job, and gets fine support from Marcus Stephens' expressionistic set (lit by Stephanie Millar), Emily McConnell's vintage costumes, and Brett Mastellar's score.

The play has its standouts, them being the Dead End Kids - Tommy, John Dixon; Spit, Russell Armstrong; Angel, Charles Filipov; TB, Dan Forster; Milty, Steve Gensler and Dippy, Joe Goldhammer. In this production of *Dead End*, the stage belongs to Russell Armstrong (Spit), he is new, fresh and the most venomous - he can spit a city block."

Besides the revivals of the play *Dead End*, there have also been two other plays about the kids, both taking place in San Francisco, done by the One Act Theatre Company of San Francisco.

The man behind both plays was Michael Lynch. His first play was *A Letter From Leo Gorcey*, which opened in May of 1981. The story of the play about Bryan, a 33-year-old living in his bedroom surrounded by photos and memorabilia of the Dead End Kids/Bowery Boys. All day long he impersonates his hero Leo Gorcey and pals around with imaginary members Huntz Hall and Gabriel Dell. His mother Helen invites a neighbor's daughter over to the house for tea and wants Bryan to entertain her. But Bryan, being terribly shy, sees this as a threat, and it becomes clear why he prefers his imaginary playmates. Bryan's only friends are his mother and his screen-world gang members.

The San Francisco Chronicle wrote that the play was "skillfully presented" and that the "characters walk a fine line between satirical caricatures and just plain silliness."

Charles Bouvier, as Bryan, was called "touching as the man/child," while Kent Minault, (as Huntz Hall) and Steve Price (Gabriel Dell) "play their parts exceptionally."

Michael Lynch's second San Francisco's One Act Theatre Company offering, *The Dead End Kid*, opened in July of 1983. It was directed by Simon L. Levy, with a musical score by Andy Kulberg (formerly of the band The Blues Project).

The Dead End Kid was based on Lynch's earlier *A Letter from Leo Gorcey*, but was a little different this time out; it was now a musical comedy. Again, *The San Francisco Chronicle* approved, stating in its review that this new incarnation was "a zany, offbeat musical comedy that explodes with wit, energy and charm" and a "must see."

The actors cast in Bowery Boy parts were Steve Cotton (Leo Gorcey), Dan Hiatt (Huntz Hall), Stephen Sloane (Gabriel Dell) and Grant Machan (Bobby Jordan).

Additional Notes:

On September 22, 1979, at the Arlington Park Horse Track in Chicago, a horse with the name "Dead End Kid" ran in the second race, with odds at 4/1. Author put down a bet of $50 to win; he did.

On February 1, 1994, the Dead End Kids were finally given a star on the Hollywood Walk of Fame. On hand for the ceremonies were Bernard Punsly; Huntz Hall; Leo Gorcey Jr. with wife Krista and their two daughters, Eden and Hayley; Brandy Gorcey-Ziesemer, husband Tom, son Alex; and David Gorcey's grandson, David Gorcey III. During the ceremonies, Leo Jr. was given a replica of the star along with Huntz Hall and Bernard Punsly. The star is located on the corner of Hollywood Blvd. and La Brea, appropriately, dead-end street.

Star on the Hollywoodm Walk of Fame.

Hall, Alex Ziesemer, son of Brandy Gorcey, David and Megan.

Trivia

(answers on page 233)

1. How many films did George Offerman appear in with The Dead End Kids and Bowery Boys?

2. In what Bowery Boy film did Bobby Jordan appear in two scenes at the same time?

3. In what Little Tough Guy film did kid actor Lester Jay have a part? His scenes were later cut.

4. The lobby cards for what Bowery Boy film shows a building with no walls, no roof, and no back, just a front?

5. In the play *Dead End* what part did Harris Berger play before taking over the part of Dippy for Huntz Hall?

6. In what film did Bernard Punsly play a golf caddie and for whom?

7. What U.S battleship did David Durand christen during World War II?

8. In what non-Dead End Kid film did Bobby Jordan and Leo Gorcey appear in together?

9. David Gorcey, Harris Berger, Gene Lowe and George Levinson had tea at The White House with whom?

10. Bobby Jordan and David Gorcey were in what films together before The Dead End Kid films?

11. In the film *Crime School* what did Leo Gorcey try to steal while talking to the judge in court?

12. In what film did Leo Gorcey say these words, "Hey, Squirrel, you wanna twirl—you do, then rap me up"?

13. What actor who became a cowboy star and a hero to kids everywhere was in a Dead End Kid picture?

14. What superhero of television fame played the part of a soldier in a Dead End Kid feature?

15. How many musical instruments could Bennie Bartlett play fluently?

16. In the James Cagney film *City for Conquest,* what parts did Harris Berger and David Gorcey play?

17. What was the working title for *The Angels Wash Their Faces* before its release?

18. Name the actor who appeared in an East Side Kid film and later appeared on the TV show *The Rockford Files* with James Garner.

19. Gale Storm, who appeared in the East Side Kid film *Smart Alecks*, was best known for what TV show of the 1950s?

20. What Hollywood fashion designer claimed to have been a Dead End Kid?

21. Billy Halop starred opposite what Hollywood legend in her first movie role?

22. Brian Donlevy said this line; "Your brother gets in more jams than The Dead End Kids." Name the film.

23. The poem "Trees" was written by what mother of an East Side Kid?

24. James Cagney and Frankie Darro appeared in the film *Mayor of Hell* in 1933; it was later remade and called what?

25. In the film *Angels with Dirty Faces*, what amount of money came out of the slot machine that Huntz Hall broke open? What else besides the money came with it?

26. *The Life of Jimmy Dolan*, Douglas Fairbanks Jr. and David Durand, was later remade as what Dead End Kid film?

27. What actor played the part of Dippy in the *Lux Radio Theater* production of *Dead End* on radio?

28. Norman Abbott directed what TV series starring Don Adams?

29. Gil Stratton became a sportscaster for what TV station?

30. What former East Side Kid later appeared in a Bowery Boy film as a boxer?

31. After appearing in the film *Jungle Gents*, what actor became the star of his own TV series, *Cheyenne*?

32. Richard Benedict, who made four appearances in Bowery Boy films, became a director for what Jack Klugman TV show?

33. What award did Huntz Hall receive for his work in the film *A Walk in the Sun*?

34. Bernard Punsly was in what other play besides *Dead End*?

35. Joe Turkel, who played the part of Johnny Mutton in the Bowery Boy film *Angels in Disguise*, worked with Jack Nicholson in what film?

36. Pamela Blake, who was Leo Gorcey's sister in the first Bowery Boy film *Live Wires*, worked with what former East Side Kid in Columbia's two-reel series *The Glove Slingers*?

37. In the film *The Angels Wash Their Faces*, what tune did Jackie Searl whistle?

38. The poster for the Gene Reynolds film *They Shall Have Music* had what words under the title of the film?

39. What Dead End Kid said these lines: "Well I dink an' I dink' an' I dink an' I can't rememba da numba. Den I rememba da building but I forget da floor. But den I check every room an' whoever she is ain't dare." What film did he say them in?

40. What actor was originally supposed to play the part of "Baby Face" Martin in the film *Dead End*, but turned it down?

41. How many times did the musical interlude "Strange Faces" appear in a Dead End Kid or Little Tough Guy film?

42. Samuel Goldwyn acquired the rights to the Sidney Kingsley play *Dead End* for how much money?

43. Huntz Hall sang the song "Boo-Hoo" in the film *Dead End*. Who wrote the lyrics?

44. While some of the Dead End Kids sang "The Prisoner's Song" in *Dead End*, Bobby Jordan played what musical instrument?

45. Gabe Dell was nominated for a Tony Award for what play?

46. Bernard Gorcey once owned a print shop in California. What were some of the things that he printed?

47. A real steamroller / shovel was used in the play *Dead End*. What had to be done before it was used in the play?

48. In the film *Angels in Disguise*, Pepe Hern (Berti Spangler) said the line "I'm gonna cut your ears off for my scrapbook!" To whom?

49. Actor Frankie Darro played the part of what Dead End Kid in the *Lux Radio Theatre* production of the film *Angels with Dirty Faces*, which aired on May 22, 1939?

50. This may be the hardest one and if you are truly a fan, you may be able to answer it. What do the words read on Gabe's shoes in this still? (Look at the still closely.)

Trivia Answers

1. 9
2. *Mr. Hex*
3. *Little Tough Guys in Society*
4. *Bowery Buckaroos*
5. Second Avenue Boy
6. *The Big Broadcast of 1938*, W.C. Fields
7. *S.S. Sepulveda*
8. *Destroyer*
9. Eleanor Roosevelt
10. Penrod
11. Pen
12. *Destroyer*
13. Clayton Moore, The Lone Ranger, *Crime School*
14. George Reeves, Superman, *On Dress Parade*
15. 5: Drums, piano, saxophone, trumpet, clarinet
16. *Ticket Takers*
17. *The Battle of City Hall*
18. Noah Beery, *'Neath Brooklyn Bridge*
19. *My Little Margie*
20. Richard Blackwell
21. Marilyn Monroe, *Dangerous Years*
22. *The Glass Key*
23. David Durand
24. *Crime School*
25. 30 cents, six nickels and two slugs
26. *They Made Me A Criminal*
27. Harris Berger
28. *Get Smart*
29. KNXT
30. Johnny Duncan, *Fighting Fools*
31. Clint Walker
32. *Quincy, M.E.*
33. Blue Ribbon Award
34. *I Love an Actress*, 1931
35. *The Shining*
36. David Durand
37. "A-Tisket A Tasket"
38. "Dead End Kid Goes Straight"
39. Huntz Hall, *Dead End*
40. George Raft
41. 10
42. $675
43. Edward Heyman
44. Kazoo
45. *Lamppost Reunion*
46. Restaurant menus and the *Police Gazette*
47. Tear down a wall, at a cost of $5,000
48. Leo Gorcey
49. Soapy, Billy Halop's role.
50. "Here's one tongue that won't talk back"

9 781593 934675